THE GRASS IS GREENER

THE GRASS IS GREENER

Finding Your True Calling
Before Its Too Late

RICHARD G. HAGSTROM

author HOUSE®

AuthorHouse™
1663 Liberty Drive
Bloomington, IN 47403
www.authorhouse.com
Phone: 1-800-839-8640

First published by AuthorHouse   08/23/2011

ISBN: 978-1-4634-4202-6 (sc)
ISBN: 978-1-4634-4203-3 (ebk)

"Above all else, guard your heart, for it is the wellspring of life"
Proverbs 4:23

"In his heart, a man plans his course, but the Lord determines his steps"
Proverbs 16:9

ACKNOWLEDGEMENT

Special thanks to Kay Coulter, who not only edited this book, but also created the drawings and illustrations. Her creativity, insights, and thoroughness are deeply appreciated.

TABLE OF CONTENTS

INTRODUCTION

WHAT THIS BOOK IS ABOUT. At one level, this book is about valuing God in your innermost being, so much so that you will want to seek Him expectantly, consistently, and patiently while making decisions.

At another level, this book is about thankfully valuing what God has given you—abilities and skills, the freedom to make choices as to your employment, the opportunity to serve Him— to name a few things He has given you.

The goal of this book is to help you to not only please God with your life and lifestyle, but also to please God by being in meaningful-to-you work at a factory, office, or while at home, taking care of the house, family members, etc. In part, this means understanding how your job and attitude towards it may either positively or negatively impact your home life, spiritual life, church life (or other volunteer work), and in general, your relationships.

For example, someone in the right-for-him or her job/work/occupation tends to have a positive attitude, to be willing to take on a variety of volunteer jobs, to pitch in at home, and to take the initiative rather than procrastinate. He or she will often have less difficulty (it is never easy!) getting along with a wide variety of people.

On the other hand, someone in wrong-for-him or her job/work/occupation tends to have a negative attitude, to be less willing to do volunteer jobs, to be less willing to pitch in at home, and often procrastinates, rather than take the initiative. He or she often has difficulty getting along with people.

So a key message of this book is that our job satisfaction, or our feelings (positive or negative) towards what we do day-in, day-out effects us not only while working, but also carries over into other key areas of life—including at home, relationships, and spiritual life.

This book will give you an organized decision process to use while you are:

- Thinking through decision options (e.g. what volunteer job to take, or whether you should take job X or stay where you are now), or
- Sorting through your personal values, or
- Figuring out what you really want to do with your life. You will really learn a "way of thinking" about such decisions, which I hope becomes an ongoing "thinking things through" process.

As we go along, we will be trying to keep God's perspective in mind with questions like:

- Will that be a God-pleasing decision?
- Are my motives pure?
- Will God be glorified?

In a nutshell, the goal of this book is to help you live out your calling from God responsibly, with God reverently and respectfully in mind. "For we are taking pains to do what is right, not only in the eyes of the Lord but also in the eyes of men" (2 Corinthians 8:21). Our witness (words and actions) is seen; we cannot hide. But our promise from God is that He will help, enabling us as He is at work in us. "For it is God who works in you . . ." (Philippians 2:13a). What is impossible with us is possible with God's help. *Thank you, God.*

So this book is not primarily about helping readers make more money, or gain powerful or more influential positions. While you may, for example, make more money as a result of reading this book, that would be a secondary outcome, rather than primary. I am more interested in encouraging readers to be living God-pleasing lives and being Godly people in every area of your lives—at work, home, church, with your neighbors, and while standing in line at the grocery store checkout counter. We are here to fulfill God's purposes for us, not our own.

WHO SHOULD READ THIS BOOK. This book is intended for two inter-related people groups. One, *people uncertain* about what they should be doing, and two, *ordinary people* who want to quietly and effectively serve God.

People uncertain are:

1. People who are at crossroads. They don't know whether to stay or leave, take job opportunity X or Y, to move or not move to a new location and new opportunity. They are in a quandary, and perhaps do not want to make another job change mistake.

2. People who have "hit the wall." Everything they have tried has not worked out. While in the past they felt they knew what they wanted to do, now they are not so sure. Uncertainty about what they really should be doing has raised its ugly head. And their confidence is spiraling downward fast.

3. People struggling, even unhappy in their present jobs. It is turning into a "grind" and more and more they are coming home too pooped to pop? "But why?" they may be asking, "I am doing what I studied in college."

4. People who are now very happy in their work, but are wondering if there is more out there for them. Or is there something more "people-helping" they should be doing? They are dead serious about wanting to live God-pleasing lives, either where they are now, or in some other job or job location.

5. People making educational choices . . . high school seniors, college sophomores, people now working but in transition and who need further education (e.g. a college degree or some type of technical education).

6. People wondering what they should DO after retiring, in order to stay active, feel productive and useful, and the like. The principles and concepts we will discuss will apply directly to such people.

In a nutshell, people reading this book tend to be in a "not-know, not-sure" mode. In your mind, you may be thinking you should know, but in your heart of hearts, you also know that you do not.

This uncertainty may be hard for you to face because it most likely involves change. On top of that, you may feel that everyone else seems to know for sure which way they are heading. At least, they give that impression and this intimidates you.

Frankly, it is my view that you should admit your doubts now. This would be a sign of strength and maturity, rather than weakness and immaturity. Lots and lots of us have gone through (yours truly included) what you are now experiencing.

You see, many out there do not know, but are not mature enough to admit it. Their heads speak confidence, while their hearts are aching. So they are crushed by the world's system which says: "Chin up . . . push hard . . . it will turn out OK."

What often happens is, many such people go on their way and drift out into the world and into a purposeless existence. But you are different. You want your life to count for something good, to make a difference, even a small difference. So when it is your time to "turn in," you will do so knowing you literally tried your best to do what you felt God wanted you to do. So I am saying it is OK to admit you don't know. It is step 1 (foundational) to finding your calling into a life that counts, from God's standpoint. This book will point out essential things you should know and need to know in order to get a handle on what direction to go. This direction will give you hope, and we all need hope.

Ordinary people. Another way of describing the group of people I had in mind while writing were 'quiet' people, behind-the-scenes people, call them ordinary people. "Make it your ambition to lead a quiet life . . . so that your daily life may win the respect of outsiders" (1 Thessalonians 4:11-12).

Ordinary people usually do not create a "big splash," or get on the evening news, or have movies made of their lives. Now do not get me wrong,

I am glad there are people who do these things. But as I wrote, I thought mainly of the needs of ordinary people, and I count myself one of them (us). We are out here "in the trenches" trying our best at being faithful followers of Christ. Like everyone else, we stumble, have good and bad days, and sometimes wish life would not be so testing and challenging.

But like the robin tilting his head to listen for a worm in the ground, so we are "tilting our heads" trying to hear God, reading His Word while not understanding all it means, trusting that somehow we are able to sense or discern what would please Him. Many, many times we are unsure, but we are sure who God is. And there is a lot we can't explain.

I believe God uses ordinary people in ordinary circumstances of life. He may have called 12 apostles, but think of all the other disciples who were not called like the 12, who labored and struggled unnoticed. You know what? That is where most of us are . . . there, in the ordinary things of life doing small, little, unnoticed acts of love on behalf of Jesus. Many times we wonder if it is worth it, but then we come to our senses, knowing He wants us to be unswervingly devoted to Him, not primarily to be "gaining notoriety," or striving to do things "visible" in the eyes of people and so be "duly" recognized.

Catch the touch of real Christianity from *Daily Thoughts For Disciples*, page 141, by Oswald Chambers (Christian Literature Crusade, Fort Washington, Pennsylvania, 1976):

> We do not need the grace of God to stand crisis; human nature and pride will do it. We can buck up and face the music of crisis magnificently, but it does require the supernatural grace of God to live twenty-four hours of the day as a saint, to go through drudgery as a saint, to go through poverty as a saint, to go through an ordinary, unobtrusive, ignored existence as a saint, unnoted and unnoticeable. The 'show business', which is so incorporated into our view of Christian work today, has caused us to drift far from our Lord's conception of discipleship. It is instilled in us to think that we have to do exceptional things for God; we have not. We have to be exceptional in ordinary things, to be holy in mean streets, among mean people, surrounded by sordid sinners. This is not learned in five minutes.

In a nutshell, this book is for people, yes ordinary people, whose love for God and devotion to Christ motivate them to "be faithful" and consis-, tently Christian day-in, day-out, with no press releases announcing to the media their next "act of love." It is not a media-attractive act, but for sure a God-pleasing act.

A GLIMPSE INTO MY WRITING PHILOSOPHY. For the past three months, I've been in a mood. I've had a bad attitude. What got me down were my abortive attempts to write this book without sounding too spiritual, as if I have "got it together" or sounding "preachy" to you the reader, in so doing turning you off.

So along with that, of course my spiritual life sagged. I restarted, restarted, and restarted writing this introduction and chapter one, intentionally trying to sound practical rather than spiritual. I felt lousy. What I wrote was dull as a doornail. It read awful. My heart was not in it.

A few mornings ago, after a lengthy prayer time alone with God, this book title came to me, as well as this introduction. Suddenly, my outlook changed, my hope restored (including that I would get this book done), and I said: "I'm going to do it my way, and if I sound spiritual, so be it." What I learned I was doing was literally leaving God out, ignoring key Scripture references, and the like. Isn't it absolutely crazy how quickly and easily we get off track? That is right, I should know better. Did Satan deceive me? Perhaps. But I think I wanted more of "my wonderful ideas" to shine through, to look "smart and practical." Yes, pride did raise its ugly head.

On top of this, sometimes I weary of asking and asking God, praying and praying, and wondering when am I ever going to be able to do it without going to God all the time. The answer? Never. Yes, I was not really praying from a heart intent on wanting God's help. Remember, I was trying to write "unspiritually" (leaving God out) and without sincere prayer in wanting God's help. Now that's a prescription for disaster!

So if you are reading this book and discouraged, I hope the ideas and concepts you will be reading about will help you see the light (your life direction) but also see The Light (God) in a more significant way.

But have realistic expectations about how God may "treat us" as ever present Guide and Helper while decision making. Yes, He is our personal Lighthouse during life's struggles and storms. While we with squinted eyes and hands pressed horizontally against our foreheads want to catch a clear "vision" of His Plan for us, God seldom does.

Instead, He keeps us at bay, going from storm to calm to storm to calm so that we will stay focused on Him, while revealing just enough of Himself and His plan for us to keep going. Is He mean? No. Does He have our best interests at heart? Yes.

So why no "clear vision" from God about tomorrow? So that we will draw on Him daily, rely on Him now, and be in a constant dependent mode (such as I am now more apt to be), rather than independent-of-Him mode (when I was trying to write "unspiritually").

In this process, we experience a deepening intimacy with God Himself. "This happened that we might not rely on ourselves, but on God . . ." (1 Corinthians 1:9). God is our Lighthouse; we are meant to be His Light (and Salt) here and now. Do we really want that? Do we really value God? Do we really want God's help? Really?

If your answer is yes, but with this qualifier: "I'm not sure I can do it," then that attitude will please God, because He will help you if you are in a "help me, God" mode. His answers may be a lot different from what you expect, His timing different from your timetable. But being faithful and often reaching out to Him for help in times of knowing and not knowing, questioning and getting answers, encouragement and discouragement will be foundational to doing what He desires for us.

"And without faith it is impossible to please God, because anyone who comes to him must believe he exists and that he rewards those who earnestly seek him" (Hebrews 11:6). His reward will include His Divine Presence in our human lives, and His Thoughts imbuing our thoughts.

SECTION ONE:

UNDERSTANDING YOUR CALLING AND WHAT GOD DESIRES

CHAPTER 1
GOD'S CALL TO EVERYONE

INTRODUCTION

Most people have a thousand and one <u>thoughts</u> zipping through their minds every 10 seconds. In jest or in casual conversation, I often ask people: "What is rattling around in your brain right now?" Most people know a lot, but our thoughts are often so disjointed we can "hear" our ideas rattling around inside our brain (hear them now!).

The *goal of this chapter* is to reduce the "rattle around" syndrome by introducing two easy-to-follow decision processes that will serve as a framework for making decisions. Its aim is to be instrumental in your BEING and DOING (these two are inseparable) what God desires for you in your particular life circumstances.

These decision-making processes have been developed with God <u>and</u> you in mind. Sound selfish having "you" in mind? Yes, but it really is not. In general terms, here is what I mean by keeping God and you in mind.

We keep **God in mind** by asking these questions about each decision:

- Will it please God?
- Will God be glorified?
- Will it be consistent with Scripture?
- Have I prayed early and often as a needy soul, wanting and desiring God's intervention, direction, or answer?

We keep **ourselves in mind** during decision making by:

- Knowing and considering our individual capabilities and strengths when choosing and doing any job.
- Knowing and seriously considering our (and others') personal values and priorities, and life purpose.
- Examining our motives to test whether or not they are as pure as possible, in God's eyes.

Now let's look at an organized decision process that does just that—keeps God and you in mind.

AN ORGANIZED DECISION-MAKING PROCESS

Tina worked in the development department of a large non-profit organization. After two and half years, she found herself losing her edge, feeling less energized—the work becoming less meaningful to her. Using the tools and concepts we will be learning, she found out she should be a graphic artist or portrait painter.

Greg was a purchasing agent for his company. He felt he should be making more money. Using the same tools as Tina, he learned he was in the right-for-him job. To pursue another higher paying job would have used his abilities less, leading to the dreaded "illness"—job dissatisfaction.

In my view, the ultimate aim of any organized decision process is to arrive at a decision that pleases God. Not only is each part or component of the decision process right, so God-pleasing . . . but the final decision should be right, so also God-pleasing. "So we make it our goal to please Him" (2 Corinthians 5:9).

Back to Tina and Greg. Don't think for a moment it was easy for them to reach the conclusions they did. It "flew in the face" of many things a secular society views OK and right for individuals. But while decision making, they followed the right process . . . it included God and themselves in the decision process. They did what was right in God's eyes.

Briefly, "pleasing God" means to live a life He approves, to look at things from His perspective, to make decisions "soaked" with Scripture and prayer. A high standard? Yes. A tall order? Yes. But if we do not hold high a standard, then we will succumb to living a less than pleasing-to-God life.

So God summons us or calls us to live pleasing-to-Him lives. It's within the context of Pleasing God that I've put together a "tool," an organized decision process that I used with Tina and Greg . . . and hundreds of other people. This organized process is two-level.

At level one, it applies to everyone universally. At level two, it applies to individuals. Level one I call (for lack of a better title!) Universal Calling, level two I call (ditto) Individual Calling. Each has three components or parts that are not mutually exclusive, but interrelate with each other. And as we will see later in this chapter, our Universal and Individual Calling also interrelate with each other. Let's look at each one . . . first our Universal Calling.

UNIVERSAL CALLING

Universal Calling means God has a call out to everyone, everywhere . . . all mankind. This decision process (see fig. 1-a) highlights what people should value in terms of relationships, commitments, and motives. Our appropriate response at each part of the decision process, coupled with the goal of doing what God desires will, in my view, set the stage for our Individual Calling.

One, pleasing God includes having a PERSONAL RELATIONSHIP WITH GOD THROUGH JESUS. "God, who has called you into fellowship with his Son Jesus Christ . . ." (1 Corinthians 1:9). John 17:3 instructs us: "Now this is eternal life: that they may know you, the only true God, and Jesus Christ, whom you have sent."

The word "know" in John 17:3 and throughout Scripture usually means a close "knowing," not a distant or casual knowing. The point is: God is pleased when our walk with Him is close, rather than casual or distant. This dimension of our Universal Calling represents our *priority relationship*. No earthly relationship should come ahead of our relationship with God. We will talk a lot more about this in the pages ahead, but suffice it to say here that God's call to everyone is to believe in Jesus and experience the indescribable preciousness of fellowship with Him.

When a parent calls the kids for supper, they should come running (if they are obedient), wash their hands and face, then sit down to eat. Similarly, God calls everyone to have dinner/fellowship with Him. We must

UNIVERSAL CALLING

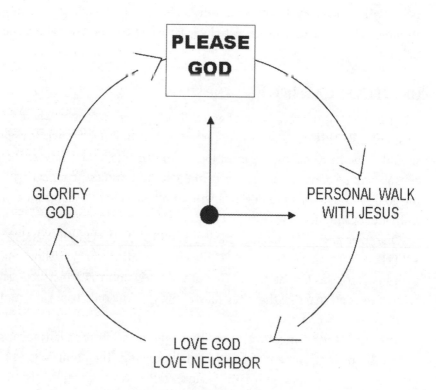

UNIVERSAL CALLING: To please God (2 Cor. 5:9): (1) Having a *personal relationship* with Jesus (1 Cor. 1:9); (2) *Loving* God and neighbor (Mt. 22:37, 39); (3) *Glorifying* God (Is. 43:7).

fig. 1-a

respond initially by "washing ourselves" by confessing our sins, asking for His forgiveness, then committing ourselves to follow Him and His teachings, as found in the Bible. In so doing, we enter into a personal relationship with God through Jesus.

We receive forgiveness because when Jesus died on the cross, He died for us. He did it because He loves us, period. I do not deserve or merit His Love. In turn, God expects us to love Him and to walk closely/intimately with Him (or have a close personal relationships with Him). When we do, He is pleased.

In the Bible, when someone commits his life to Christ, he is called a "new creation" . . . from that point forward, he enters a totally new world of values, relationships, goals, and the like. "If anyone is in Christ [believes wholeheartedly in Christ], he is a new creation; the old has gone, the new has come" (2 Corinthians 5:17).

It is God who does the changing; a transformation takes place that changes me into a new being. The "new has come" includes new goals, new friends, new priorities, new motives, new attitudes, and the like. And that kind of change usually does not happen overnight! It takes a lifetime. Now to the second dimension of our Universal Calling, our priority commitment.

Two, when we LOVE GOD and LOVE OUR NEIGHBOR, we are pleasing Him. When a person starts a relationship with another person, there is usually something about them they respect or admire. Almost unconsciously he or she will commit themself to them . . . to spend time with them, do things with them or for them, and the like.

At its ultimate meaning, valuing God means to love Him without reservations and wholeheartedly. It pleases Him when we do. "Love . . . God with all your heart and . . . soul and . . . mind . . . Love your neighbor as yourself" (Matthew 22:37-39). This dimension of our calling represents our priority *commitment*.

And what will be the result? "If you love me, you will obey what I command you" (John 14:15). That obedience will include "loving our neighbor." One thing I do often at the beginning of my quiet time is to tell God I love Him. I repeat it several times for my benefit; it reminds me what my first love should be. For me at least, it is so easy to forget God (as hard as that is to admit), and let Him slip to second or third place in my commitments.

If my priority commitment is to love Him, then I'll be more apt to virtually unconsciously obey His Word (assuming I'm a student of the Bible) and be doing what He desires, even though I may not consciously know I'm doing it.

In other words, because you and I love and respect God, we will demonstrate our love by spending time with Him and so get to know Him better—grow closer to Him, as well as do things He desires (obey His Word).

Then as His Love permeates our being, you are empowered to love your neighbor . . . the person next to you and meet his or her needs. God should be our first-love . . . not our lawn, job, kitchen, or favorite automobile. And this task is not for the "timid-hearted." It takes huge amounts of discipline and commitment.

So the first two "ingredients" of our Universal Calling are to 1. enter into a personal relationship with God through Jesus, and 2. to continue growing that relationship by making a commitment to love Him and love our neighbor. As a result, God is pleased. Now to the third ingredient of our Universal Calling, Glorifying God—our motives.

Three, GLORIFYING God as we do things pleases Him. ". . . Whom [you and I] I [God] created for my [God's] glory . . ." (Isaiah 43:7). Think of that. He made us in the first place to bring honor and glory to His Name, not my name. This dimension of calling covers our *motives*. So whether deciding to purchase a car, make a job decision, or standing in line (already late) at the grocery store, my decisions, conversations and things I look at or do are done with a view of representing Jesus there.

He didn't create us to eat. He created us to be God-glorifying people in order to Please Him. "So whatever you do, do it all for the glory of God" (1 Corinthians 10:31). We do things with God in mind, not primarily ourselves in mind. So why am I "laboring" writing this book? The answer: To glorify God. To a large extent, God-glorifying motives spring from a grateful heart that acknowledges all we are and have comes from a loving God who created us for His Glory.

A "motive" is something within a person, not without them, that prompts action. It literally warms the "cockles" of my heart to think that some people might read this book and so study their Bible more, or think more of God while decision making, or find out how their job will effect their "walk with God." I trust these are God-glorifying motives . . . that is, as a result of they doing these and other things, they too will please and glorify God more.

And Jesus said in John 5:30 (and similar things elsewhere in John): "For I seek not to please myself but him (God) who sent me." If Jesus' statement does not stop us in our tracks and cause us to evaluate (and correct) our motives, nothing will.

Let's *summarize* this Universal Calling section. When someone out there, chatting with a friend, leans forward and says to him or her, "I haven't found my calling yet," he or she usually means they have not figured out yet what direction to go in their life, or they have not yet "found their niche" . . . a place where they would be happiest. In general conversation, calling often refers to job. Such a view, while true as far as it goes, is only part of, but not the complete way to view our calling. While job is important, and will be so viewed in this book, it is not everything there is to life.

As I hope you are seeing, from God's viewpoint, there is a far more important calling, and that is to please Him in EVERYTHING that we do. Right relationships, right commitments, right motives (as just described) go a long way in God's eyes.

So "Making Decisions with God and You in Mind" begins first by being deadly serious about God, and then making the appropriate commitments, adjustments, and changes as we make life's decisions and face life's problems. In a nutshell, first and foremost we are called to God, not to an occupation.

Unfortunately, not everyone acknowledges God. So rather than trusting and embracing God and His Promises, they trust themselves and other gods (e.g. education, money, etc.). Their rejection does not change the fact that our Universal Calling is to God Himself, and when we commit ourselves to Him, His Divine Presence fills a deep spiritual void in us.

Our Universal Calling is really a way of thinking about God's role and place in our decision making. I hope this organized process lifts your eyes upward, softens your heart and attitude, and resets your motives. Our appropriate response to God (as just described in the Universal Calling process) opens the way to another (second) level of calling, our Individual Calling.

INDIVIDUAL CALLING

Next we'll briefly describe our Individual Calling (Figure 1-b)—briefly now but comprehensively as we go along in later chapters. So for now, here is a brief overview, starting with what is meant by Individual Calling.

INDIVIDUAL CALLING

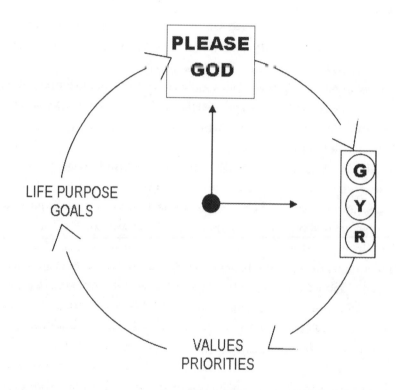

PLEASE GOD

LIFE PURPOSE GOALS

G
Y
R

VALUES PRIORITIES

INDIVIDUAL CALLING: To please God (2 Cor. 5:9) through: (1) *Using* one's Strengths (Greens) and some Limitations (Reds) (Eccl. 5:18-20); (2) *Realizing* one's Values and Priorities (Eph. 4:1); *Achieving* one's Life Purpose and Goals (Heb. 13:16 TEV).

fig. 1-b

The Individual Calling is how we as individuals go about "living out our Universal Calling" . . . the specific things I do or don't do, say or don't say, value or don't value, embrace or don't embrace. Again, my goal is to do what God desires of me, and so please Him. "Live a life worthy of the calling you have received" (Ephesians 4:1).

Here are the three interrelated components of this Calling process; they are essential decisions to getting insight into what a person should do to please God.

1. An understanding of our God-Given <u>STRENGTHS/CAPABILI-TIES</u> (Greens . . . explained shortly) and our God-Given <u>LIMITA-TIONS/LIMABILITIES</u> (Reds . . . explained shortly). In turn, we are to responsibly use the talents or "gifts" He has given us while "living out our calling." In chapter3, we'll show you how to discover your Strengths (Greens) and Limitations (Reds).

2. An understanding of our <u>VALUES-PRIORITIES</u>. Values-Priorities represent what we believe important and significant in our lives. Examples might include family life, growing and maturing mentally and spiritually, aging parents, meaningful/purposeful job life, church life, physical conditioning, and the like.

3. A understanding of our <u>LIFE</u> <u>PURPOSE</u> and <u>GOALS</u>. In a later chapter, we will be defining Life Purpose as the people a person wants to be helping, as they are using their Strengths (two paragraphs above) and realizing their Values (above paragraph). We will look at Goals as a way of realizing our heart aspirations.

So if a person has an understanding of these three things, he or she is more apt to DO and BE (applying and carrying out) what God desires for him or her individually.

THE UNIVERSAL UMBRELLA

We "hold high" our Universal Calling. It keeps us focused . . . eyes on Who is most important. With that in mind, we place ourselves and our Individual Calling within the umbrella—"protection" and "influence" (positive) of our Universal Calling (Fig. 1-c).

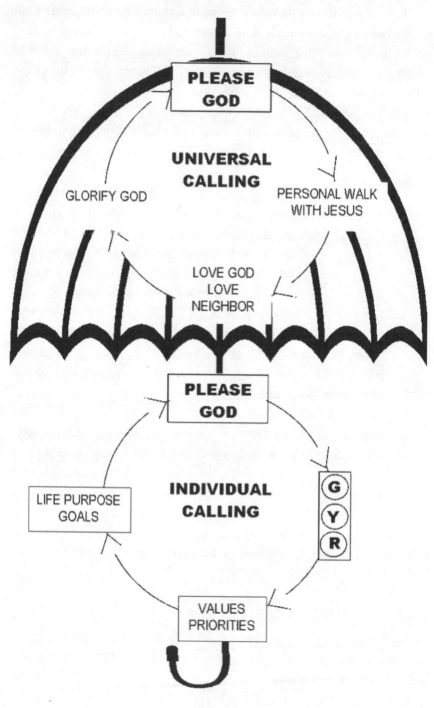

fig. 1-c

Said differently, our two Callings work together. Our Universal Calling readies or prepares us, putting us in direct contact or a personal relationship with God via His Son Jesus. Then God continues working in us (Philippians 2:13) as we live out and apply our understanding of what God desires for us.

WHAT FOLLOWS

In nutshell fashion, what follows in this book falls into two sections. Section one is "Understanding Your Calling and What God Desires." It lays the foundation for Section two. Section one content will include discovering your Strengths (Greens) and Limitations (Reds), clarifying your Values-Priorities, and thinking through your Life Purpose and Goals.

Section two is "Living Out Your Calling and What God Desires." This will be mainly the application side of things . . . applying concepts of this book to job life, home life, volunteer life (including church life), spiritual life, and briefly to student life.

The aim will be to help a person do well in life, from God's perspective. While job life occupies a major place in life, hence a big time consumer, relationships, spiritual life, home life, etc. are also integral to our overall "success." So while job is very important, life is significantly more important.

Before heading out into discussion of the Green Light Concept, Chapter 2, let's pause for a moment, and think of needs that you and others may be facing. Keep these needs in mind as you are reading and thinking how concepts in this book might assist you and others you are helping/mentoring and encouraging in the days ahead.

WE ARE NEEDY PEOPLE, AT LEAST SOME OF US ARE!

Perhaps today you (or someone you know) find yourself in a quandary; it is unsettling. While tomorrow always involves uncertainty, your uncertainty is going "overboard." In fact, your self-confidence may be slipping away, out of control. People have a wide variety of needs this book addresses. Here is a sampling of them:

Age, late 30s: "I'm at a crossroads, not knowing if I should stay where I am or take another position. I've never answered the question 'What should I be doing in life?' Been too busy, I guess."

Age, late teens, early 20s: "I have no idea what I want to do or what to major in. Some days I think there's something wrong with me." A college freshman says; "I'm thinking about so many possibilities . . . they all sound interesting and 'cutting edge'. But I'm confused."

Age, mid-40s: "I'm dry. I have no energy and drive. I'm feeling tired and worn down and discouraged."

Retiree: "I'm bored stiff, and at times feel depressed. I feel useless most of the time."

Age, late 20s: "I'm drained. Even with my Master's Degree, I'm finding little meaning and purpose in this job, and lately in my life. What's wrong . . . I got A's in my major while at college."

Age, early 50s: "I'm down. I started a business, but my relationship with my business partner soured. Spiritually, I'm at zero. The joy of the Lord is gone. I have to force myself to go to church and see my 'happy' friends."

Needs and problems come in all shapes and sizes. People of all ages experience frustration, especially job-related frustration. So if you are frustrated, you are not alone. Sure, every job has its up days and down days, but after a while, how you really feel about your job will rise to the surface. Yes, including yours truly.

I graduated from engineering school. I hated college, "squeezing" by on C's, and a few B's (very few). I hated my first job—design engineer. I lasted 18 months.

Then I went from the proverbial frying pan into the fire. I took people's advice and made a major change . . . into sales. I hated calling on people. I felt like a wooden duck making the sales presentation. I detested closing the sale—asking people to buy the product now, today and not tomorrow. Pressure, pressure!

But no one would listen to my frustrations, especially my manager. They said: "Dick, sales is where the money is. And if you want to move up in the company, this is the way. Dick, you've got what it takes."

I experienced everything people in the above examples felt . . . bored, lacking energy, no drive or zip, and no place to turn. I was directionless, no life focus or direction. I was at a crossroads.

Universal Calling? Individual Calling? Such concepts never crossed my mind. Please God? Never gave it a thought. While I believe I was living a moral and ethical life, in retrospect I wonder today if I was a believer then, one who was trusting God every day. I doubt it. For many years I "wandered around" in a spiritual desert; during that time, God graciously had mercy on me until I came around (really, came to my senses) in my late 30s, making a serious, from-the-heart commitment to Christ.

BUT WHY?

Why do so many people end up in some "frazzled and frustrated" state or in a "not knowing what to do" situation? While many people admittedly seem to always "land on their feet," that has not been your experience . . . mine either.

Why? Of course, potentially there are many reasons, but in my view they have (usually unintentionally) left God and themselves out of their decision process. And most likely they did not use an organized decision process. I sure didn't when I was "in the muck" going from design engineer into sales.

So we fall into the trap and entanglement of the secular system with such concepts as "work hard and you'll succeed," "the right education is key to success," "know the right people," "do things to make your resume look good," and the like. You can make a case for each one of these right now. They are not necessarily bad, but from God's viewpoint, I believe not good enough. Most of the people I deal with who come to me "frazzled and frustrated" admit they have naturally slid into the secular system of "success." More about that later on in the book.

CHAPTER SUMMARY

We fallible, sinful people have a knack for doing things our way, rather than God's way. Our decision processes at best are half-organized, if not totally unstructured.

The Universal Calling process which makes God central in our decision making, and the Individual Calling process which brings you into the decision process, are both designed to help you cover the right bases, so not leave out key decision components.

Both are interrelated, on-going processes, so inseparable to someone whose deepest desire and aspiration is to do what God desires, and so please Him.

In the next two chapters, we will deal with one component of the Individual Calling process, our Strengths and Limitations . . . starting with Chapter 2, You.

CHAPTER 2
YOU

INTRODUCTION

The *goal* of this chapter is to look at you the individual, keeping in mind the concept of "Making Decisions with God and <u>You</u> in Mind."

By keeping "you" in mind, I mean you in terms of your strengths and limitations while decision making. Your strengths are what you or any other individual will tend to do well and get job satisfaction from doing it well.

Limitations are what you or any other individual will tend not to do well and get little or no job satisfaction from doing it. As just described, all people have their individual strengths and limitations. Almost everything we do uses a strength or limitation, except laughing, crying, and slipping on ice!

We will also look at "you" from God's viewpoint and why your strengths and job satisfaction level are so important, especially as they impact on your relationships and spiritual life.

We begin now a more comprehensive look into each part of the Individual Calling process, namely by understanding a person's individual strengths and limitations. Looking now at the Individual Calling process, fig. 1-b. We are at the three o'clock position . . . the big hand points to God, the little hand points to you.

INDIVIDUAL CALLING

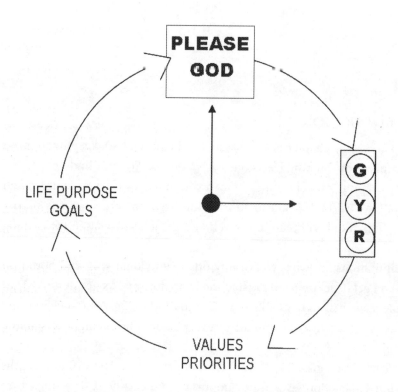

INDIVIDUAL CALLING: To please God (2 Cor. 5:9) through: (1) *Using* one's Strengths (Greens) and some Limitations (Reds) (Eccl. 5:18-20); (2) *Realizing* one's Values and Priorities (Eph. 4:1); *Achieving* one's Life Purpose and Goals (Heb. 13:16 TEV).

fig. 1-b

TRAFFIC LIGHTS AND YOU

Traffic lights use Green, Yellow, and Red signals to communicate a message to motorists, who are expected to use and obey the signals while going from place to place. Now think of traffic lights as a way of viewing people through the lenses of Green, Yellow, and Red signals. The strengths/limitations idea is communicated quickly using this analogy. People usually prefer Green lights to Red lights!

A person's Greens represent his or her strengths, Yellows and Reds his or her limitations. Now let us describe each one.

<u>Greens</u> represent two interrelated things: one, a person's skills—the things he or she will tend to do well (at A or B+ levels), and two, the satisfaction or sense of accomplishment he or she receives from doing something well. See fig. 2-a.

When people understand that a project or task will use their Greens, they will usually look forward to doing it (didn't say they would not get nervous or be stressed a bit beforehand) and so "go" (Green signal)—take the initiative, take action.

For example, my Green skills include analyzing/problem solving (don't be too impressed!), consulting or advising, and teaching as a facilitator. When I do (action) these things, I receive job satisfaction from "doing them right" or "righting what was wrong."

Another person's skills may include building relationships, helping/encouraging, and socializing/visiting . . . and get lots of satisfaction from "brightening" someone's day or lifting another's spirits.

Someone else's skills might include conceiving new ideas, designing, and producing a visible-to-the-eye end-product like a painting or window display, or room interior, getting lots of satisfaction from the creative process itself and producing an eye-appealing end-product.

Another person's skills might include directing a large organization, promoting large events, and inspiring people, getting lots of satisfaction from seeing an organization grow or making it more profitable.

All people have strengths, and these vary from person to person. By knowing "you" in terms of your strengths—skills and what gives you job satisfaction, you will have invaluable information to use during decision making. More about that shortly. Let us look now at the other side—a person's limitations—his or her Reds.

THE GREEN LIGHT CONCEPT*
♦ SATISFACTION
♦ SKILLS

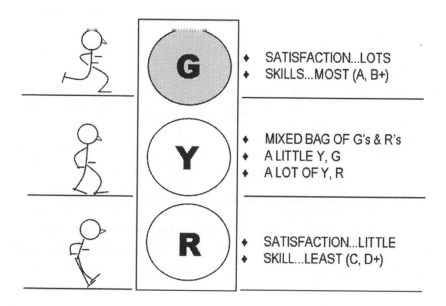

♦ SATISFACTION...LOTS
♦ SKILLS...MOST (A, B+)

♦ MIXED BAG OF G's & R's
♦ A LITTLE Y, G
♦ A LOT OF Y, R

♦ SATISFACTION...LITTLE
♦ SKILL...LEAST (C, D+)

*Considering only time-consuming, on-going responsibilities and reasonably responsible, mature people.

fig. 2-a

Reds also represent two interrelated things, but quite different from Greens. One, Reds represent a person's limited skills—things they will tend not to do well (at C or D+ levels) and two, what will give them limited or no satisfaction or sense of accomplishment from doing it. See fig. 2-a.

Unlike looking forward to doing a Green, a person anticipating doing a Red will tend to hesitate, or put off starting it in the first place, or come up with a thousand and one reasons why he or she should not do it (in a later chapter we will deal with how to responsibly do Reds, rather than not do them). Overstating the case, Red means "stop." However, to repeat, I am not saying at any point we should not do Reds.

My Red skills include (don't get depressed!) selling, promoting, directing a large organization, to name a few! I get no satisfaction from making a sale, or inspiring people, or being instrumental in an organization realizing its profit goals.

A key point: as we think about Greens and Reds, we are considering *only* TIME-CONSUMING, ONGOING (day-in, day-out) responsibilities, not once-a-month or five-minute projects. So a person may do a Red well (A or B+ levels) if it involves brief stints rather than four or five hours daily. So keep this in mind throughout our discussion of Greens and Reds. Now for a brief look at Yellows.

Yellows are a mixture of Greens and Reds, so exercise caution. A person can usually do a Yellow somewhat effectively (like Green), but with a major caution—in small amounts. The other side is, doing long stretches of a Yellow at one time usually becomes distasteful to a person, resulting in less effective performance (like Red). So exercise caution: some Yellow, fine; six straight days of Yellows? No.

A Mini-Summary

Greens represent skills and satisfaction; Reds represent less skill and satisfaction. Green signals "go," Red signals "stop." When people see Green, they usually "step on it" (take the initiative). Looking ahead to Red work, people usually naturally "put on the brakes" (slow down or stop). We will be discussing this a lot more as we go through this book.

THE GREEN LIGHT CONCEPT AND YOU

Your Greens, Yellows, and Reds are key aspects of YOU, as they relate to "Making Decisions with God and *You* in Mind." So in the context of this discussion, it would be accurate to say: "Making Decisions with God and your Greens, Yellows, and Reds in Mind."

This means a person is most apt to be effective (do well), be productive (achieve expected results), and get job satisfaction (sense accomplishment) day-in, day-out when the *heart* or *core* of his or her daily responsibilities uses his or her Greens. In a nutshell, the goal of thinking about people via Greens, Yellows, and Reds is to help them do well—something I am sure pleases God.

Of course, Reds are also part of every job and everyday life. We will discuss this later in this chapter under the heading "No Perfect Job, All Greens."

THE PHILOSOPHY BEHIND THE GREEN LIGHT CONCEPT

Here are six principles and beliefs that UNDERGIRD the Green Light Concept.

1. God _wants_ and _expects_ you to be satisfied.

We have just said a person's Greens include what gives them job satisfaction. Did you know that God's Word instructs us to be satisfied? Notice Ecclesiastes. 5:18-20: ". . . It is good and proper . . . to find satisfaction in . . . toilsome labor."

I bet you have never really noticed verse 20, which tells us the by-product or result of a person's being in satisfying-for-him or her work: "He seldom reflects on the days of his life, because God keeps him occupied with gladness of heart." The first time I read that verse, my jaw dropped. I noticed a direct connection between job satisfaction and gladness of heart. God is surely keeping us in mind, giving us gladness of heart. The question is: are we keeping Him in mind?

Think of it. It is OK (good and proper, vs. 18) to like what you do. Not only that, God expects it. God, who created you, did so desiring that you be satisfied. He is asking you to find satisfaction in your work. That is your part.

If you are satisfied, then He (not you or anyone else) will keep you occupied with gladness of heart. That is God's part.

No wonder the author also wrote (Ecclesiastes. 3:13): ". . . That everyone may . . . find satisfaction in all his toil—this is a gift of God." Think of that! Satisfaction is a gift, and best of all, a gift of God. But can you believe it?

Satisfied people "whistle while they work" (well-l-l-l . . . at least part of the time!). God graciously gives them "glad hearts." And they work hard . . . they "toil" (See again Ecclesiastes 5:18-20 and the words "toilsome labor"). Work is work, not a picnic.

Looked at differently, God created people with an inner need for receiving satisfaction from what they are doing. As used in this book, satisfaction means internal-to-the-person feelings of accomplishment. It is an intrinsic reward . . . the right kind of pride for having "toiled" hard and done something well (A or B+ levels).

So does being satisfied and doing something well please God? Yes. Does being dissatisfied (including grumpy, even bitter) and doing C or D+ work displease God? You answer that one.

As used here, the word satisfaction does not imply complacency, status quo, coasting, and the like.

In a nutshell, when we "find satisfaction" (Ecclesiastes 5:18), we are literally respecting, carrying out, and so meeting an important Biblical principle: God wants and expects you to be satisfied (in your work).

2. *All people have Greens and Reds.*

This may sound simple to say, but surprisingly (at least to me it is) there are a lot of people "out there" who believe differently. A college junior said to me: "I have always felt I had the potential to do anything I wanted to do."

What he was saying is similar to what lots of others say (whether they actually believe it is a different matter): "With hard work, a good attitude, and loads of determination I can do anything they give me to do." And it may be true, someone might be able to do almost anything, but I ask, at what cost?

If these philosophies happen to land people in their Greens, fine. On the other hand, as happens to lots and lots of people, if they end up in Red jobs, a potential disaster is in the making. These are just some of the high cost consequences: negative stress; burning the candle at both ends; burnout; and the like. More about that shortly.

In a nutshell, the Green Light Concept asks you to accept the notion that a person has both Strengths/Greens, and Limitations/Reds. And with all the erroneous "stuff" out there saying "you can do anything," then the Green and Red Concept may be a struggle for you to accept. At one point in years past, I felt there was not much out there I could not do.

I clearly recall the time I realized I was not a manager, which I then defined as one who runs or directs a large department, division, or company. Up to that point, I thought I had the potential to be a manager—at least most people whose opinions I respected said that.

I had at times pushed myself to become a manager; at other times, my interest in doing that waned. It was like a breath of fresh air to accept and understand my Greens and Reds. In my heart of hearts, I knew it (that I was not a manager), but had been programmed to think that being a manager was the only way to be successful.

It was reassuring to know my Greens and Reds, then build my life direction around who I am, not around who I am not (manager). We all have Greens and Reds.

3. Greens and Reds are God-given gifts to everyone.

Here we are talking about our skills, our natural talents or natural "gifting." Everyone, I repeat everyone—male or female, believers or non-believers, have been gifted by God. "It is he [God] who made us, and we are his; we are his people . . . ." (Psalms 100:3).

In other words, in creating us, He gave us both Greens and Reds, not just Greens. The particular mix of Greens and Reds He gives us is His decision, not ours. He created us. Why He does things this way is His decision, period. So a person really does not know why he or she has Greens, like creating and designing, and Reds like public speaking and selling.

What we do know is any gift giver expects the gift receiver to be grateful and put it to good use, rather than stow it away. Similarly, God expects us to say "thank you," to be grateful receivers and responsibly put them to good use while living out His calling for His glory. "Whom [people] I created for my glory . . . ." (Isaiah 43:7).

So God's call to us individually is to responsibly use our Greens <u>and</u> some of our Reds—both, not one or the other. As we have already said, every job has Reds. So rather than fret about what we do not have in terms of Greens, we should be giving our attention to what we do have, Greens and Reds.

In other words, people should accept their Greens, Yellows, and Reds, and trust God. Trust that He made us just as we are for reasons known mainly to Him. So in this book, we will view our Greens and Reds as one among many of God's gifts to us.

In a nutshell, our Greens and Reds are both God-given. The question we should be asking ourselves is whether we are grateful receivers of His gifts and grateful to Him for the way He made us, rather than asking why He did not give us certain Greens or wishing He gave us Greens He never intended for us to have.

4. There is <u>no perfect job, all Greens.</u>

Almost every Green job includes Red things to do often. In other words, there is no perfect job (all Greens). As Pat said: "As a homemaker, there are things I want to do (Greens), and things I have to do (Reds)." "Want to" and "have to" go together.

Part of our Individual Calling is to responsibly use our Greens <u>and</u> some of our Reds. Repeating, God made us AND gave us our Reds, not just Greens. And as we said, He expects us to use what He has so graciously given us.

To make this "No Perfect Job" concept more concrete, consider the 40-20-40 Concept. It is my view that at least 40% (more would be nice!) of what a person does should be Green-using—to enable them to be satisfied, energized like a car, fueled for action.

Then 20% of their work should be Yellow, the rest, 40% Red. Now if this ratio is 60% Green (rather than 40% Green) with fewer Yellows and Red, so much the better. The exact percentages are not what is important. What is important is that responsible people be doing things they want to do and have to do (Thank you, Pat Homemaker).

Reds come with the territory. We do not have to go around looking for Reds—every job has them. So, for example, a pastor may get lots of satisfaction from preparing a sermon, doing things like researching, studying, pondering, writing it, etc., but get little satisfaction from delivering the sermon to a large audience. Or vice versa—a pastor may get lots of satisfaction from speaking, but little from preparation, like researching, etc.

A teacher may love teaching but hate correcting papers or disciplining students. A social worker may get satisfaction meeting with clients, but no satisfaction from doing the required paperwork.

As conscientious believers, it is our responsibly use our Greens and some of our Reds; in other words, do our best consistent with our abilities. Said differently, it is irresponsible on our part to avoid or duck unpleasant (Red) jobs. "Don't always be trying to get out of doing your duty, even when it is unpleasant" (Ecclesiastes 8:2-3 TLB). We will be discussing "Dealing with Reds" in chapter seven.

Summarizing this "No Perfect Job" concept, there may be times in life where a person, out of necessity, must do Red work (say 90% of his or her job) for an extended period of time. For example, he or she might take a high-paying Red job to pay off unanticipated medical bills or simply to gain experience to qualify for a Green job down the road. But these should be the exception, rather than the rule. In the long run, and from God's perspective, He expects us to practice balance and intentionally do our best to responsibly do Green work and Red work.

5. _There is a Green Magnet within_.

A magnet draws paper clips towards itself. We see the effects, but we do not see the forces pulling it. Similarly, a person's Greens tend to pull us or draw us towards doing Green work. For example, if a person has a choice between baking cookies and cleaning the house, if their Green is baking and Red is cleaning, he or she will tend to naturally gravitate towards baking cookies.

Or if I am faced with teaching a class or fixing an electrical motor, I would be drawn towards teaching, my Green. I want to hasten to add here that I am not saying we automatically do the Green thing at hand. I might just have to do the Red. All I am saying is our Greens act like a magnet, drawing us to do our Greens. Why? Because that is what will give us satisfaction, or sense of accomplishment.

In a nutshell, our Greens represent a strong tendency, not a controlling force on our behavior. Often our initial impulse is to want to do our Greens, even though we know in our heads that is not the thing to do right now. So, recognize that you have a Green magnet within, which we will identify specifically in the next chapter.

One more point—while we have this internal Green Magnet within, we should not push this concept too far. Why? God is our Master Magnet; recognize that He is continually drawing us to Him. "No one can come to me [Jesus] unless the Father who sent me draws him . . . ." (John 6:44). Mysterious? Yes. Real and experiential? Yes. People may resist His draw or respond in faith to it and so enter into a personal relationship with Him (fig. 1-a, Universal Calling). God, like a magnet, is always pulling at people.

Bringing together the two magnets . . . the Green Magnet functions within the broad umbrella of the Master Magnet (fig. 1-c). We march to His beat, not the other way around. "Since we live by the Spirit, let us keep in step with the Spirit" (Galatians 5:25). Our Greens do influence us, but His Spirit should be the dominant influence in our lives.

6. *Decision Latitude*

While I respect people who may have different views about how God interacts with a person during the decision-making process, it is my view that God usually gives us both the freedom and responsibility to decide our future—that is, where and how to best use our Greens and some of our Reds for His Glory.

I say this with this important qualification. That is, as we are making decisions, we depend (literally and totally) on God by asking for His Spirit (Luke 11:13), and His Wisdom (James 1:5)—as we make choices about what field to go into, what job to go after, what education to pursue, what life values to be embracing, what kind of people needs to be meeting, what to be doing as a volunteer, how to handle our money, etc.

All said differently, God's Plan is to help you make a best decision. He does not have a specific, detailed plan for your life. His most important plan for you and me is that you love Him wholeheartedly and have a close walk with Him.

Thinking mainly of life direction now, you and I have to figure out our life direction, where to live, etc., in this process making what we hope and desire is the best decision . . . God-pleasing and being in a field or job that counts. As a result, you may end up with two or three options, within a general direction. For example, I am a Tasks person (the meaning of which will be explained in the next chapter).

As such, I could have gone into the teaching field, professional speaking field, or consulting field; I chose the latter. And then within consulting, I had to choose from several possibilities, finally deciding to concentrate on churches, para-church organizations, businesses, and individuals.

Here is the point. I don't think God is going to "slam the door to heaven" because I did not choose teaching. Nor do I think He is displeased with my consulting choices.

Do I know for sure? No. Did I follow what I believe was a God-pleasing decision process? Yes. So do I feel called to consulting work? No. I feel called to live in fellowship with God, and then called to use my Greens and some of my Reds in a responsible fashion in my chosen field, which turns out to be consulting.

Many times in life I have wished God had written me a memo to tell me what to do or reassure me that what I chose was right. But He has not done that yet! But He has chosen to work with His creatures in a give-and-take relationship, like a partnership. He always does His part; I falteringly do my part. He loves me; I do my best to love Him with my whole being.

The closest thing I get in memo form from God is when He nudges me or creates a hunger in me to read His Word more, or pray for those I have said I would pray for, or to "get away" for a time to meditate, think, and pray, or to telephone or go see so-and-so, etc. I don't need to label or categorize these nudges. I just need to do them.

God gives us latitude because He wants us to love Him because we want to, not because we must. He wants volunteers, not soldiers. He values friendship, not military-like obedience. Our obedience is unconscious, our actions springing from a servant heart.

Summarizing: these six principles represent the thinking behind the Green Light Concept. I hope they point out or affirm the "find satisfaction in your toilsome work" principle, and help you understand how important it is to have enough Green in what you do.

We have expressed the idea that God did not create robots He programs to "crank out" decisions about life, work, etc. Instead, He created people with minds, ideas, wills, abilities, emotions, and the like. So our decisions are not programmed. In cooperation with God, each person must decide, using a God-pleasing decision process.

THREE KEY BENEFITS

Why does a person really have to make the effort (next chapter) to discover their Greens and Reds? Is it not it enough to know them generally, rather than specifically, or what they might be, rather than know them for sure? Well, I would like to advance three benefits which I hope will encourage you to "pin down" your Greens and Reds. While not the only benefits, they are key ones. So by being aware of their specific Greens and Reds, a person can usually . . .

1. Form realistic (and accurate) expectations.

That is, before a person does something, he or she can form both realistic and accurate expectations about how well he or she will most likely do something. So people can anticipate doing Green-using responsibilities fairly well and getting satisfaction from doing them; and conversely, expect to do Red-using responsibilities not too well and get little or no satisfaction from doing them.

So I can expect to do consulting (my Green) fairly well. Every time? Most likely not, because I might have planned it wrong, or the client did not prepare, or the timing of the consultation call poor, etc. But these are the exception, not the rule. So I can expect to usually do well while consulting at a client's location.

Now—about my Reds. I, like you, do not want to do inferior work, but instead quality, excellent work. Since I can expect to not do Reds well (C or D+ levels), if my goal is A or B+ work, it means I have to prepare for and do Reds differently; that is, in my planning, preparation, and doing of it, not treating it like a Green, but treat it like it is, a Red. In Chapter 7, we will deal specifically with that issue and how to do that.

2. Erase false guilt.

The dictionary defines guilt as "the feeling of responsibility for some offense, crime, etc." By the way, only responsible people feel guilty. The word "responsible" means (from dictionary): "to hold oneself accountable for his decisions-actions." Responsible people "hold themselves respon-sible" for "not measuring up," or not doing something well, so they experi-ence guilt. To them, because they are responsible people, their guilt feelings are genuine.

Have you ever felt guilty for not liking to do door-to-door solicitation, or getting uptight and feel tongue-tied in front of 300 people to make a simple five-minute presentation, or getting all nervous and confused lead-ing a small group Bible study, or not being able to express yourself well in conversation?

This guilt is real if you believe (which I do not) that with enough prepa-ration and with the right attitude, a person can do anything. Well, believe what you will, but you should *not* feel guilty because, in all probability, what you are trying to do and do well is a Red. If so, the guilt you are experienc-ing is not really true, but false.

Lots and lots of people come to me feeling guilty and burdened by their lack of desire to socialize and mix with people, or build deep relationships with people. In virtually every case, what they are guilty about involves one of their Reds.

Do not misunderstand. I am not suggesting or implying that you should not do any of the above. All I am saying is you should not feel guilty for not "measuring up." You don't measure up because your standard and expecta-tions are unrealistic. Remember, we usually **do** Greens well and **do** Reds not so well (C or D+).

While we will be discussing this more in Chapter 7, "Dealing with Reds," suffice it to say now that by forming more realistic expectations (because it is a Red), a person doing a Red will often feel little or no guilt, enjoy the task more (even though it is a Red), and be more apt to sense a wee bit of satisfaction or accomplishment while doing it.

It is enough to feel guilty about our sinful attitudes and behavior with-out also heaping on feeling guilty for not measuring up after doing a Red.

3. Understand the Impact (of Greens and Reds) on Relationships.

This is the BIG benefit, the effect Green work and Red work have on relationships. Look at fig. 2-b, "By-Products." The left side lists the effects of a person's being in Green work, the right side the effects of someone's being in Red work. A reminder: we are considering only time-consuming, ongoing responsibilities, not two-minute tasks. Item 7 on the chart addresses relationships.

So someone doing Green work will tend to be upbeat, energized, and positive at work, at quitting time, and during his or her non-work time at home. On the other hand, someone doing Red work all day long will tend to be downbeat, totally de-energized and negative at work, at quitting time, and during his or her non-work time at home. This applies to at-home parents as well, except there is no quitting time!

Who would you rather spend time with, Greenie or Reddie? The point is: someone satisfied tends to have the potential for good people relationships (potential because of all the variables that effect relationships like level of maturity, common sense, motives, etc.); someone dissatisfied in his or her work will tend to have the potential for poor relationships with people.

Now to the BIG, BIG benefit, head and shoulders above all others. That is, not only are our people relationships impacted but I have also discovered, after working with hundreds of believers over the years, that our RELATIONSHIP WITH GOD or WALK WITH GOD is also impacted. See fig. 2-c.

In a nutshell, this means if a person is in Green work, he or she tends to have the *potential* for a close walk with God. On the other hand, if he or she is in Red work, there is less potential for a close walk with God. As such, the intimacy is gone . . . personal Bible study and prayer becomes mechanical. This kind of person begins thinking there is a spiritual problem or he or she is not totally committed to God.

BY-PRODUCTS

BY-PRODUCTS	BY-PRODUCTS
Green: Most effective Most productive	Red: Less effective Less productive
BY-PRODUCTS of GREEN work	BY-PRODUCTS of RED work
A person is most apt to be ... 1. Satisfied 2. Decisive 3. Positive (attitude) 4. Self-starter, doer 5. Organized 6. Cooperative 7. (Have) Positive relation- ships, using his best people skills 8. Hopeful/excited 9. (Have) Positive stress 10. Team player/contributor 11. (Have) High energy 12. (Find) Meaning and purpose from work.	A person is most apt to be ... 1. Dissatisfied 2. Indecisive 3. Negative (attitude) 4. Procrastinator 5. Disorganized 6. Less willing, reluctant 7. (Have) Negative relationships or not-so-good people skills 8. Gloomy-down 9. (Have) Negative stress 10. Withholder 11. (Have) On-again, off-again spurts of energy 12. (Find) Little meaning and purpose from work.

Keep two things in mind as you read the above: (1) many situational variables impact performance, like the quality of supervision, relationships, training, working climate/atmosphere, realism of expectations, etc.;

(2) the person will impact his own performance. For example, his level of
maturity, motives (good or bad), ethics, morals, common sense (or lack
thereof), and the intensity of his commitment level.

fig. 2-b

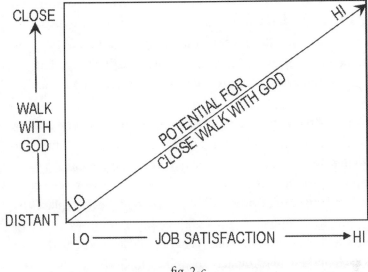

fig. 2-c

I recall vividly having lunch with a senior pastor of a large church. On the drive over to lunch, he told me he had listened to a tape; it confirmed in his mind that his commitment to the Lord was less than it should be. As we talked, he "unloaded." His Mondays to Wednesdays were in his words "just awful." He said: "I am fighting depression." The upshot was he was in a Red job. Then we had a healthy discussion about why his walk with God had lost its richness and intimacy. He said: "This concept has put a totally new light on the problem I am facing."

So we often "cool" towards God because we are in Red work too much (there are many other valid reasons, of course), with little or no satisfaction from our toil. Green work is like fuel to a car—it energizes. Red work is like running on an empty fuel tank, or running on fumes—no energy, no zip, no life. Is this God-pleasing? No. I believe an often overlooked contributing cause for people not walking closely with God is that they are in Red work.

Repeating, Green work is like fuel to a car—it energizes. A person desiring to walk closely with God is energized to read his Bible, to pray, etc. In turn, he tends to be "alive" and more apt to be "salt and light." Is this God-pleasing? Yes.

On the other hand, Red work is like running on an empty fuel tank, or running on fumes... no energy, no zip, no life. Even to a person desiring to walk closely with God, the Bible becomes heavy to lift, prayer time becomes almost meaningless and perfunctory. Is this God-pleasing? No.

In my view, a significant dimension of our spiritual lives should be a close walk with God. And whatever interferes with or negatively impacts that walk is our *enemy*. It must be faced, attacked, and remedied. That includes Red work.

So is it worth it to be in a high-paying Red job and not be walking with God as you know you should? The answer for me is a resounding "No." And is it worth it to be in a low or lower paying Green job and be walking as you know you should with God? The answer for me is a resounding "yes." No "dream house" or "dream this or that" should ever replace the most important relationship—our walk with God. Money must not dictate our lifestyle, life choices, life decisions. What should be dictating these matters is how each of these may impact our walk with God.

Please don't push this next thought too far, but think about it in a general sense. Job satisfaction (high or low) tends to be the "tail that wags the dog" in that it effects so many vital dimensions of our lives, especially relationships. See again fig. 2-b, "By-Products." Looked at positively, high job satisfaction has the potential to convert good intentions into concrete action. Looked at negatively, low job satisfaction has the potential to be like concrete around our feet and minds, making it hard to move ahead.

I believe that these three benefits give you good reasons to discover your Greens and Reds. If not actually discovering them for the first time, then at least let them affirm or confirm what you may already know about yourself.

A "SPLITTING HAIRS' CHAPTER SUMMARY

We have learned from Ecclesiastes 5:18 that God wants and expects us to find satisfaction in our work. You and I know there are other sources of satisfaction besides job satisfaction. They include values-priorities satisfaction or realization. So if one of your values is family life, and that is crumbling, it hurts. When you are realizing a good family life, it adds to your overall life satisfaction.

Similarly, our spiritual life realization or satisfaction impacts our overall life satisfaction. So when our walk with God is personal and peace giving, we find satisfaction from the quality of our spiritual life.

While it may seem obvious when I say this, we often unintentionally overlook the fact that the source of our job satisfaction is the job itself— what we DO there. The source of our spiritual satisfaction is Jesus . . . His Divine Life in us. The source of our values satisfaction in the above illustration is quality family life.

Here is the point. The answer to a job satisfaction problem (low satisfaction) is the job. To increase satisfaction usually involves changing responsibilities. Jesus is not the answer to a job satisfaction problem.

However, Jesus is the answer to our spiritual problems. No Jesus—no spiritual satisfaction, no vitality, no hope. Let me quickly add: Jesus and His Holy Spirit will enable and help someone on the job (Green), or help in the process of changing to Greener, more satisfying work. But do not expect Jesus to do what only the job can do.

I realize I am splitting hairs, but I do want to keep these sources of satisfaction separate, especially job satisfaction from spiritual satisfaction. I have too many people coming to me in Red jobs trying to spiritualize the solution, much like the senior pastor we just talked about. No, the cause for feeling so dissatisfied about a job most likely is not a spiritual issue; most likely it is a job issue. I repeat: the primary source of job satisfaction is the job itself.

I am splitting hairs because it is impossible to separate job, spiritual, and values satisfaction; they interact and interrelate to each other continually. But I hope the "splitting hairs" process helps put what each one is and supposed to do into perspective.

Now let's find out how to discover a person's Greens, Yellows, and Reds. The next chapter is more than just reading; it includes writing some things down as part of finding out specifically YOUR skills and what gives you job satisfaction. Remember: your personal satisfaction is one of God's gifts to you (Ecclesiastes 3:13). He wants you to experience that. He will not keep it from you. "No good thing [like satisfaction] does he [God] withhold from those whose walk is blameless" (Psalm 84:11). So as you read Chapter 3, I hope you will take an extra few minutes to pinpoint what will give you job satisfaction.

CHAPTER 3
Your Greens and Reds

The *goal* of this chapter is to show you a way to discover YOUR Greens and Reds. To do this, you will use a proven-in-practice, quick-to-do process, including tools and helps to do this accurately so you will have confidence in your conclusions.

REVIEW AND INTRODUCTION

In Chapter 2, we learned the BIG, BIG benefit of knowing Greens and Reds is its potential impact on our walk with God. Too much Red work carries with it the potential for a distant, rather than close walk with God. And being in Green work carries with it the potential for a close walk with God, if we will exercise sufficient discipline to desire that for our Christian lives.

With this in mind, let's look briefly at a few dangers of a distant walk with God. They include:

- Less inclined to hear God when He tries speaking to us
- Less desire to want to read His Word and obey its instructions to us
- Less likely to deal decisively with sin that is always creeping into our lives
- More likely to depend on ourselves, rather than on God and His Holy Spirit

These are just a few. You can think of many others. In contrast, some of the benefits of a close walk with God include:

- More likely to hear God—be sensitive to what He would want and so better discern His promptings or checks (or lack of peace about something).
- More likely to trust Him . . . really trust Him, from the heart.
- His Word will become alive, motivating, and encouraging . . . so we are more apt to obey its instructions.
- Increased desire to constantly do things that please Him.

Again, these are just a few benefits. You will think of many more. These alone should be reason enough to want to know our Greens and Reds so that we have the potential not only to experience His Presence in deepening ways, but also be more apt to be a prepared, ready to act as ambassadors of His on the bus, at home, in the car, at the dentist, etc.

In Chapter 2, we also learned two key ingredients of our Greens and Reds were satisfaction and skills. They go together like hand and glove. So a person has Green satisfaction and Green skills, and Red satisfaction and Red skills.

Scripture is clear: "Find satisfaction in your toilsome work" (Ecclesiastes 5:18). "Find" implies there is something for which to look. So we must look for satisfaction. It stands to reason to *find* anything, you must look in the right place. If I want my car keys, and they are in a coat pocket in the front closet, no amount of searching in the kitchen will turn up the car keys. I will find them only in my coat pocket located in the closet. In a moment, we will learn the right place to look for our areas of satisfaction and skills is in our life's Positive Experiences. First . . . a quick intro to the concept of Positive Experiences.

WHAT HAVE THEY DONE?

When a person is being evaluated for a job, college, etc., the person evaluating him or her usually looks back at his or her record. Implied in what the person does is the thought: "What has he (or she) done?" In this way, a person finds out his or her level of experience, areas of interest, things he or she has done well, etc.

We are going to do the same thing—look back and ask: "What have I done?" Since we are looking specifically for satisfaction and skills, we will not look at just any experiences, but experiences you have had that were satisfying to you, and that you did well (skills). In this way, we will be using a structured or organized process to help us to look in the right place (as in finding car keys in my coat pocket in the closet) and surface the right information.

The right place to look is in what I call life's Positive Experiences. Fig. 3-a lists my life's Positive Experiences. First, let's describe what we mean by a Positive Experience.

POSITIVE EXPERIENCES are things a person has done in the past, which gave him or her a sense of *accomplishment* or *satisfaction*. These experiences may have occurred at any time—at home, during school, at work, while pursuing a hobby, and so on. Specifically, a Positive Experience is any past experience that a person wanted to do because they:

- Were <u>naturally</u> <u>interested</u> in it
- <u>Desired</u> doing it
- Did it <u>fairly</u> <u>well</u> in his or her opinion
- Sensed <u>satisfaction</u> or <u>accomplishment</u> from doing it

Positive Experiences are really "qualified" past experiences—qualified by the previous (underlined) four criteria. Since we are interested in finding out a person's skills and satisfaction, we simply ask him or her to identify experiences he or she has had that they did well and gave them satisfaction. Yes, it sounds simple, but the process will develop the right information.

Examples of Positive Experiences literally run the gamut; here's a sampling: making friends at school; solving math problems; doing research at the library; working at present job; starting a business; leading a small group program at church; fixing computers; being treasurer of XYZ company; building houses; being a stock broker; selling X product; designing promotional programs for clients; taking care of a golf course.

POSITIVE EXPERIENCES LISTING SAMPLE

A Positive Experience is any past experience that you wanted to do because you:

- Were naturally interested in it
- Desired to do it
- Did it fairly well, in your opinion

A Positive Experience gives you a sense of accomplishment or satisfaction. Divide your life into two parts (approximately half each): Time Period I and Time Period II. Time Period I begins at age 5. Time Period II ends at the present. So a 30-year-old would include experiences from ages 5 to 17 in Time Period I and experiences from ages 18 to 30 in Time Period 2.

Also try coming up with two or three Positive Experiences that occurred in the first half of your Time Period I. In the "30-year-old" example, the first half of Time Period I (age 5 to 17) is ages 5 to 10 or 11.

TIME PERIOD I	TIME PERIOD II
1. Giving memorized talks at our church, about 5th grade.	1. Consulting calls on companies, problem solving.
2. Learning to shift and drive a large dump truck.	2. Directing management schools and being one of the instructors.
3. Giving valedictory speech, 8th grade.	3. Problem solving with individuals, churches.
4. Listening to students' problems. They would often call me.	4. Being a visiting lecturer for colleges.
5. Instructor in school for new sales people.	5. Putting an addition on our house; making furniture.
6. Instructing (or speaking) at weekend retreats. Also did a lot of 1-on-1 problem solving with people between times	6. Putting together on-going self-development programs.
7.	7. Doing in-company seminars

fig. 3-a

So from hundreds of life's experiences, a person picks out a dozen or so experiences that meet the above criteria for a Positive Experience. Everyone's Positive Experiences are different and unique to them. No one else knows them, so it's up to each person to develop his or her own list. "Each heart knows its own bitterness, and no one else can share their joy" (Proverbs 14:10).

When completing this Listing, I usually suggest a person divide his or her life in half, starting at age 5 or so. In this way, he or she is sure to cover almost all of their remembered life experiences without missing or overlooking certain segments of their life. Then he or she should list 5 to 7 Positive Experiences for each half of his life. If someone wants to list more, that's fine.

You will benefit most from this book if you will take time right now and jot down your life's Positive Experiences on a separate sheet of paper. I have also included a form (see fig.3-b) you may use for reference.

As you recount your life's experiences, keep referring to the definition of a Positive Experience and the four criteria. You will find experiences "jumping out" at you. Write them down. This is a fun exercise for most people. It is usually best to list what pops into your mind right at first. Some people do this in 25 minutes; others like to take more time.

After completing your listing of Positive Experiences, you have (or will have) in front of you experiences that gave you satisfaction, and what you did fairly well—areas of skill. To make this information most useful, we need to go from the general—the listing you developed, to the specific—discovering and identifying what it is that gives you satisfaction, and your particular skills.

DISCOVERING YOURS GREENS AND REDS PREVIEW

We will be learning shortly that there are four primary sources of Satisfaction for people; one of these will tend to be their Green (primary source) which gives them lots (or the most) of Satisfaction. The other three sources will be either their Yellow (some Satisfaction) or Red (little or no Satisfaction).

YOUR POSITIVE EXPERIENCES LISTING

A Positive Experience is any past experience that you wanted to do because you:

- Were naturally interested in it
- Desired to do it
- Did it fairly well, in your opinion

A Positive Experience gives you a sense of accomplishment or satisfaction. Divide your life into two parts (approximately half each): Time Period I and Time Period II. Time Period I begins at age 5. Time Period II ends at the present. So a 30-year-old would include experiences from ages 5 to 17 in Time Period I and experiences from ages 18 to 30 in time Period 2.

Also try coming up with two or three Positive Experiences that occurred in the first half of your Time Period I. In the "30-year-old" example, the first half of Time Period I (age 5 to 17) is ages 5 to 10 or 11. Circle these earliest two or three.

TIME PERIOD I	TIME PERIOD II
1.	1.
2.	2.
3.	3.
4.	4.
5.	5.
6.	6.
7.	7.

fig. 3-b

A person uses his Positive Experiences Listing to identify his Green Satisfaction source as well as his Green Skills. In other words, within us "lay" our Greens. It is up to us to uncover them and so discover Greens and Reds.

I would like to PREVIEW this discovery process via four different Positive Experiences to illustrate what we will be doing and how we will do it, assuming each Positive Experience is from a different person.

Positive Experience A: Starting and building an organization to 600 employees. What gives Satisfaction? Reaching the organization's key success indices like sales, profits, growth objectives, etc. Using what Skills? Directing (or managing) a large organization and promoting the company and its products. We will be calling this type of person a **Strategy** person.

Positive Experience B: Organizing space for clients, making things a lot more efficient. What gives Satisfaction? Making improvements, straightening out messes. Using what Skills? Organizing space and fixing/upgrading systems and procedures. We will be calling this type of person a **Tasks** person.

Positive Experience C: Designing wall murals and designing pictures for clients. What gives Satisfaction? Producing a visible end-product or creating beauty. Using what Skills? Creating/designing and drawing/painting. We will be calling this type of person an **Ideas** person.

Positive Experience D: Building relationships with volunteers; coordinating the volunteer program. What gives Satisfaction? Developing close relationships with people and helping out. Using what Skills? Building relationships and coordinating volunteers. We will be calling this type of person a **Relationships** person.

To repeat, Positive Experiences give information about Greens—both Satisfaction and Skills. And as you most likely have already discerned, what specifically satisfies people usually differs from one person to the next.

As you will soon be seeing, I would get no satisfaction from directing a large organization. So *Strategy* is my Red. I am so thankful I know this about myself. How do I know this for sure? By conclusions I reached after going through this Discovery process.

A second chance! If you have not already done so, stop now and jot down some of your life's Positive Experiences. They will prove themselves to be instructive to you the rest of your life, if you will use them. I think about and refer to mine often. They continue to help me (three benefits, end of Chapter 2). These three benefits are:

- Form realistic expectations
- Erase false guilt
- In my relationships, especially with God, but also other people.

So much for the PREVIEW. It is time now to figure out what gives YOU satisfaction and the skills you use while receiving satisfaction. I will explain the Discovery Process, using myself as the example. In this process, you will be naturally thinking about how it applies to you and your Positive Experiences.

SATISFACTION

The goal now is to discover what gives you Satisfaction. So with your completed Positive Experiences Listing in hand, compare what you did in your Positive Experiences with the information in Fig.'s 3-c through 3-f. Each page describes four different types of people in terms of areas in which they will tend to be most effective, productive, and satisfied.

A <u>STRATEGY</u> person tends to focus on strategies and tactics that produce: (1) rapid large (300+ people) organization <u>growth/profit,</u> or (2) sales to individuals or groups of people or audiences, or (3) <u>wins</u> over a "worthy opponent," or (4) <u>believers/supporters</u> for an idea or proposition.

1. **DIRECTING** Large (300+ Organization)

1. **SELLING** hard-to-convince buyers

1. **COMPETING** in highly competitive settings

1. **SPEAKING** before large (500+ audiences)

Receives **SATISFACTION** from: Reaching key success indicators/goals for a large (300+ people) organization like sales, profits growth/expansion; winning over hard-to convince people or tough opponents.

fig. 3-c

Examples of **STRAGEGY** POSITIVE EXPERIENCES

Example 1

- Winning foot races against neighborhood kids
- Stood up to older kids bothering my friends
- Sold books door to door
- Starter, top scorer on basketball team
- Age 18, sold advertising space

- Took survival course, climbed mountain in winter
- Making sales against difficult odds
- Coaching our team to #1 in the league
- Developing my sales territory rapidly
- Coming out #1 in sales contests

Example 2

- Recruited kids for neighborhood club
- Age 9, campaigned for local politician
- Gave speech to 300 people
- Winning debates
- Put together 10-year plan for my life

- Turned around a failing company in 9 months
- Negotiating new purchasing contracts
- Speaking at large conventions
- As plant mgr., beat all production records
- Recruited and managed 6 top performers

WILL USUALLY
Push himself and others to achieve or produce more than previously.

CHARACTERISTICS
Tends to relish outdoing a worthy opponent or overcoming people's resistance to an idea or proposition, while outwitting, outmaneuvering, competing, debating, or selling; loves the contest and the mental combat while "dueling" with people in highly competitive situations; winning or coming out near the top tends to be primary goal.

fig. 3-c(2)

A **TASKS** person tends to *focus* on the task itself and doing a specific step, routine, operation "by the book" so: (1) something is <u>organized, orderly, neat</u>, or (2) something runs <u>right</u> or is <u>built right</u>, or (3) something is handled/completed <u>accurately</u> or <u>right,</u> or (4) while troubleshooting or training there are noticeable <u>improvements</u> in equipment, people, or organizations.

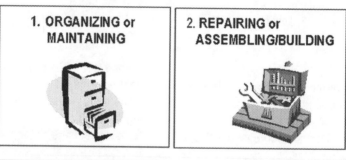

Receives **SATISFACTION** from: Doing every project step right; straightening it out or making it right.

fig. 3-d

Examples of **TASKS** POSITIVE EXPERIENCES

Example 1	Example 2

- Stacking books so neat and orderly
- Cleaning garage, mowing grass, shoveling snow
- Doing carpentry work for dad
- Building model cars
- Building cedar chest

- Painting by-the-numbers pictures
- Learned to write letter perfect
- Becoming proficient with bow and arrow
- Doing wallpaper jobs myself
- Becoming proficient at using office machines and computers

- Learned to do printing; liked fixing the machines
- Organized travel plans for a group tour
- Office administrator; organize projects, like the paperwork and details
- Enjoyed doing the paperwork when a dorm resident assistant
- Organized a stockroom so orderly and more efficient

- I repaired a motor and toaster
- Doing mechanical drafting; designing tools
- I made a cat stand with used lumber
- Teaching courses on time management
- Started an effective quality control program at XYZ company

WILL USUALLY

Keep something running smoothly by:

- Following steps/routines to a T
- Following schedules, procedures unswervingly
- Using/handling equipment correctly

Fix it by:

- Locating the malfunctioning parts
- Finding cause for the breakdown
- Training or advising someone

CHARACTERISTICS

Tends to zero in on one project; usually follows written or mental (mastered by them) checklists; tends to get overwhelmed if too many projects on the burner at once (or if too many projects thrown at them at once).

fig. 3-d(2)

An **IDEAS** person tends to *focus* on suppositions, theories, philosophies, or design ingredients/materials or style/color/audio combinations in order to: (1) produce new concepts or understanding, or (2) make an appealing design or new product, or (3) enlighten readers or listeners, or (4) bring about a pleasing end-outcome (e.g. multi-media presentation) for viewers/listeners.

Receives **SATISFACTION** from: Making new discoveries or acquiring new/more understanding/comprehension; producing a visible/audible end-product.

fig. 3-e

Examples of **IDEAS** POSITIVE EXPERIENCES

Example 1   Example 2

- Read over 500 books, age 9-13
- Learning to appreciate and love nature
- Writing poems and short stories
- Taking advanced math, coming up with mathematical formulizations
- Liked English class, especially writing

- Drew a picture of my sister
- Drawing a wildlife scene, 5th grade
- I thought up plays which my friends and I acted out
- Won an advertising contest (ad layout)
- Making a mural

- Wrote articles that were published
- Going to library, getting information, studying and understanding concepts
- Teaching literature to college freshmen

- Getting A's in art class
- Made an award-winning scrapbook
- Drawing illustrations and cartoons
- Designed a macramé vest
- Set a slide show to music

WILL USUALLY
Use mediums (words, color combinations, illustrations, formulas, etc.) that go into a "media" like a painting, product design, stage production, TV commercial, musical composition, information system, etc.

CHARACTERISTICS
Tends to become engrossed in the learning or creating process while thinking reflectively, imagining, or creating; often loses track of time while pondering an idea/concept; savors the learning or creating process—sights, sound, smells, tastes, or touch—experiential in nature; relishes beauty, harmony, or sense of balance and order; artistic; cerebral.

fig. 3-e(2)

A **RELATIONSHIPS** person tends to *focus* on individuals, teams, or groups in order to (1) build relationships or help out, or (2) restore confidence or help out, or (3) reassure or enlighten them, or (4) bring about a group effort or special occasion, e.g. anniversary.

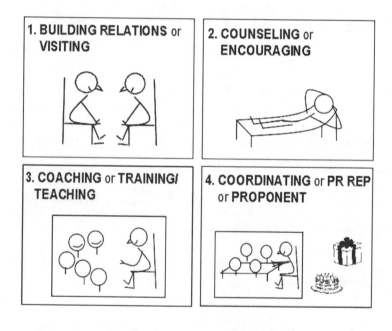

Receives SATISFACTION from: providing people/helping services or special services/helps; building relationships; being part of a group effort.

fig. 3-f

Examples of **RELATIONSHIPS** POSITIVE EXPERIENCES

Example 1

- Being a helper to my neighbors, ran errands for them
- Made desserts for my family
- Walked 20 miles, March of Dimes walkathon
- Being with friends on different sports teams
- Did volunteer work at a hospital

- Living with four people, enjoyed working things out together
- Helped a blind person cook dinner
- One of two in charge of dinners for a day camp
- Led a study with two other people
- Coached some appreciative sports teams

Example 2

- Having good times with my family
- Being well-liked by my uncle
- Making new friends at school
- Good 6th person substitute on basketball team
- Spending summers with friends, being together, becoming better friends

- My friends and I were in charge of social activities for a youth group
- Counseled troubled neighborhood kid
- Associate dean—counseled students and resident advisors
- Singing in a choir
- Being helpful and supportive to my spouse

WILL USUALLY
Pay attention to people—their plight, needs and desires, while encouraging, helping and reassuring them.

CHARACTERISTICS
Tends to relish direct one-on-one contact with people (within reason) and extending his hand of welcome, care or reassurance; often likes doing something spur-of-the-moment or being spontaneous; tends to enjoy the "hum" and camaraderie of a team or group of people working together towards common goals; may tend to thrive on new experiences, especially traveling to new locations or making an occasion fun and special for people.

fig. 3-f(2)

Four types of people are described—Strategy, Tasks, Ideas, and Relationships. At the top of the page is a one-paragraph description of each type of person. The four illustrations represent what they usually do in the process of being satisfied; right below that is a brief summary of their source of Satisfaction ("Receives SATISFACTION from:").

Additionally, "Examples of POSITIVE EXPERIENCES" gives you examples of typical Positive Experiences of these four types of people. Notice how different they are from each other (recall the same thing from our PREVIEW, a few paragraphs back). So in an IDEAS person's Positive Experiences (Fig. 3-e), notice things like writing, designing, etc. A RELATIONSHIPS person's Positive Experiences (Fig.3-f) include things like building relationships, counseling, etc.

At the bottom of the page, "WILL USUALLY" represents usual ways that type of person will do something. "CHARACTERISTICS" summarizes each type's (Strategy, Tasks, Ideas, Relationships) tendencies.

These pages are designed to help you figure out whether your Green is Strategy, Tasks, Ideas, or Relationships. To do this, COMPARE what you *mainly* did in your Positive Experiences with what you see being done on these four pages.

Look under Strategy, Tasks, Ideas, and Relationships and the four pictured Skills under each one. Ask yourself:

IS THAT WHAT I MAINLY DID IN MY POSITIVE EXPERIENCES?

- If your answer is "Yes, I did that quite a bit," then that is your Green.
- If your answer is "Yes, but I did only a little or some of that," then that is your Yellow
- If your answer is "No, I didn't do anything like that," then that is your Red.

When I did this, I asked myself, "Did I do anything Strategy-related in my Positive Experiences?" No I didn't, so Strategy is Red. In other words, I did no directing of large (300 plus people) organizations in my Positive Experiences, neither did I do any selling (I hate selling anything!), competing (I feel sorry for those who lose . . . I can't even watch the Olympics on TV), or speaking to large (500 plus people) audiences. In my Positive Experiences, I spoke to groups of 75 or less.

But Tasks is a different story—my Green. I see things there (Fig. 3-d) that look similar to what I did in my Positive Experiences. And I did a lot of trouble shooting and instructing in my Positive Experiences.

So what gives me Satisfaction? Simply doing it right, being accurate, straightening out messes. I get zero satisfaction from things that give satisfaction to Strategy people (I have no interest in winning).

Let us look for a moment at Relationships (Fig. 3-f). They "Receive SATISFACTION from" helping people and building relationships. Their mindset or focus is usually interacting with people or simply, yet profoundly, helping people. I do nothing like that in my Positive Experiences . . . so yes . . . Relationships is my Red.

I looked at Ideas (Fig. 3-e) and concluded I did some researching in my Positive Experiences, so Ideas is my Yellow. I get some satisfaction from learning new things, but I get ten times more satisfaction in my Green Satisfaction area—doing something Task-related and doing it right.

As I am sure you have already thought, there is a bit of each of these tendencies (S, T, I, R) in most people; however, one will stand out as their primary (Green) Satisfaction source.

Remember, the goal of this process is not to label you, pigeonhole you, or limit your potential; instead, only to identify specifically what gives you job Satisfaction. In turn, it may help you understand yourself a little better.

And we should not forget, only God completely understands us. So if this process raises our understanding of ourselves from 25% to 40% understanding, that is good. That will help. Never try to completely understand God's very own creation. That is His territory, not mine.

In a nutshell, one of these four types (S, T, I, R) will be your Green, one (or two) your Yellow(s), the other(s) Red(s). If you want more detailed information about Satisfaction and what people say gives them satisfaction, look at Appendix B.

Now write your conclusions below (or on separate paper) indicating your Green, Yellow, and Red tendencies whether S, T, I, or R.

Green:

Yellow:

Red:

Some people find it instructive to also write out in their own words what gives them Satisfaction.

SKILLS

The goal now is to discover your Skills. So with your completed Positive Experiences Listing in hand, glance through all your Positive Experiences. As you do this, look for similar things you did like making friends, or designing room interiors, or repairing motors, or maintaining lawns or buildings, and the like. You should come up with three or four different things you did (Skills) during your Positive Experiences.

So look at your Positive Experiences and ask yourself:

- *What did I do specifically two or more times (better yet three or more times) in my Positive Experiences?* **Your Greens**.
- *What did I not do in my Positive Experiences?* **Your Reds**.
- *What did I do just once in my Positive Experiences?* **Your yellows.**

To help you in the Skills Discovery process, look at the Skills Discovery Guide, Fig. 3-g. Notice that the Skills listed on the left are the same as the four pictured Skills in exhibits 3-c through 3-f. This Guide points out how S, T, I, and R will usually be most effective.

Look at the first four Skills—Directing through Speaking. Notice first that if someone's Positive Experiences included directing an organization of say, 100 people, then directing a small to medium-sized organization would be one of their Greens. This also means in all probability they are either T, I, or R.

SKILLS DISCOVERY GUIDE

This Guide is designed to help you pinpoint your Skills while assessing what you did in your Positive Experiences; it points out how S (Strategy), T (Tasks), I (Ideas), and R (Relationships) are usually most effective. Rely, however, on what you did in your Positive Experiences, not this Guide. Information in the left column assumes using that Skill in a time-consuming, on-going responsibility.

1. S usually effective...

1. Directing large (300+ people) organizations
2. Selling hard-to-convince buyers

3. Competing...winning a primary goal

4. Speaking before large (500+ people) audiences

T,I,R usually effective...

1. Directing small to medium (up to 300 people) organizations.
2. Selling when little to some convincing required, so tends to function in role of problem solver, prompt follow-up, etc.
3. Competing when winning a desirable or secondary goal, but not primary goal.
4. Speaking before small to medium (up to 500 people) audiences.

T usually effective...

1. Organizing or Maintaining
2. Repairing or Assembling/ Building
3. Operating/Handling or Controlling
4. Troubleshooting* or Instructing/Training*

*Step-by-step, how-to focus; moderately complex

S,I,R, usually effective...

1. Doing a little or some of #1
2. Doing a little or some of #2

3. Doing a little or some of #3

4. Doing a little or some of #4

(cont. on next page)

fig. 3-g

I usually effective...

1. Researching an area in-depth
2. Designing...inventive/original concepts

S,T,R usually effective...

1. Doing a little or some of #1
2. Doing a little or some of #2. Usually more effective designing when lots of inventiveness/originality not required; instead, while designing, making changes/modifications/improvements on existing designs.

3. Writing** or Teaching**
4. Producing or Performing
**Comparatively (highly) complex subjects

3. Doing a little or some of #3
4. Doing a little or some of #4

R usually effective...

1. Building Relationships or Visiting
2. Counseling or Encouraging
3. Coaching*** or Training/ Teaching***

S,T,I usually effective...

1. Doing a little or some of #1

2. Doing a little or some of #2
3. Doing a little or some of #3. **S** usually more effective doing #3 if winning primary goal; **T** usually more effective doing #3 when subject area moderately complex; **I** usually more effective doing #3 when subject area highly complex.

4. Coordinating or PR Rep/ Proponent
***Primary goal is skill-building, helping/advising, encouraging

4. Doing a little or some of #4

fig. 3-g(2)

The point is: while S is usually more effective directing a large organization, T, I, and R are usually more effective directing either small or medium sized organizations, assuming that is what they are doing in some of their Positive Experiences.

Or if a person did selling in his or her Positive Experiences, but where lots of persuasion was not required, then he or she would include selling as one of his or her Greens.

Dropping down to the next four Skills—Organizing through Troubleshooting, while Tasks people may do lots of this (as discovered from their Positive Experiences), S, T, and R may be effective doing a little or some of these things, but it should not be a time-consuming responsibility.

Similarly, for the next four Skills—Researching through Producing. A word of explanation about Ideas people is needed here. Usually they do best dealing with comparatively complex issues/problems, etc. On the other hand, S, I, and R are usually more effective dealing with moderately complex subjects, or how-to subjects.

To illustrate, when problem solving, Ideas types will tend to be more effective using comparatively complex problem-solving processes, S, T, and R will tend to be more effective using comparatively straightforward, step-by-step processes.

For example, those who often do well solving complicated mathematical problems using "blackboard" long (sophisticated) formulas and advanced concepts tend to be Ideas people. So while a lot of people may do OK with basic algebra, calculus, etc., Ideas people usually do best as the problems become more complicated. So in college, yours truly (Tasks) had difficulty with differential equations (somewhat advanced math), but whizzed through high school math (comparatively simple, straightforward problem solving).

The last group of four Skills—Building Relationships through Coordinating should be self-explanatory.

Now, write your conclusions below (or on separate paper), indicating your Green, Yellow, and Red Skills. Most people come up with three or four Greens, one or two Yellows, and several Reds.

GREENS: YELLOWS: REDS:

Summarizing this Satisfaction and Skills section, our life's Positive Experiences are literally a gold mine of information. We will be referring to them throughout this book, using them as an information resource and decision sounding board.

FOUR GUIDELINES

To help you reach accurate conclusions about your Greens, Yellows, and Reds, here are four guidelines to tuck into your thinking:

1. RELY on information from your Positive Experiences.

What I am urging you to do for the purposes of identifying your Satisfaction and Skills is to rely on your Positive Experiences, rather than what other people may have expressed to you in the past. Other people may have made observations about your personality or where they feel you fit, etc. Or you may have taken tests to indicate certain tendencies. Here is the point. Our purpose here is very specific—to identify what gives you Satisfaction and the Skills you will use to be satisfied. This is not personality related or based on impressions you make with people.

So someone may say: "You are so good with people, you must be Relationships." I am often told this (well at least once a year), but my Positive Experiences tell me differently. Let me assure you, it is by God's Grace that I may be good with people at times (more about this later on).

Or someone may say; "You have so many good ideas." Our point here is: you may have lots of good ideas, but your Positive Experiences may not point you to Ideas, but to say, Tasks or Relationships.

In a nutshell, rely on your Positive Experiences. It is the right place to' look to discover your skills—what you will tend to do well, and satisfaction. So put other people's comments in perspective. Thank them for their judgments (good, of course!) or compliments, but use your Positive Experiences as your primary information resource when pinpointing your Greens, Yellows, and Reds.

2. *DISTINGUISH between skills-satisfaction and personal values.*

Everyone should value people. We are often reminded that people are important. Or we read things like "people first" (before, for example, program). In other words, in everything we do, we must not overlook or "walk over" people; said differently, a priority personal value should be people.

Relating this to Strategy, Tasks, Ideas, and Relationships, does this mean only Relationships people really value people, while Strategy, Tasks, and Ideas do not value people? No, a hundred times no.

The point is this information is not a statement about your values or priorities, especially about how much a person values people. For example, Relationships is my Red, but this does not and should not say one iota about whether or not I value or love people. All of us, regardless of our S, T, I, and R tendencies should value people.

All this is saying is that if someone functioned in Red work most of the time, he or she would be comparatively ineffective, unproductive, and dissatisfied. So if I worked in my Reds all day long, in my case, working directly with people (Relationships my Red), I would be an unhappy worker. Or if a creative writer (Ideas, their Green) mainly did office administration (Tasks, their Red), he or she too would be an unhappy worker.

Repeating: The Green Light Concept is useful in the area of skills and satisfaction, not in addressing the issue of personal values. I mention this now because many people may misidentify themselves, calling themselves Relationships because they value people, rather than identify themselves otherwise (S, T, or I) based on their life's Positive Experiences. They do this thinking to not be Relationships borders on being un-Christian (Don't laugh, many people have said this to me). So do not confuse what we are doing in this chapter with your desire to help people. We will deal with the "helping people" issue in future chapters.

3. *BE YOURSELF, not someone else.*

Fred, owner/president of a 35-person firm, completed his Positive Experiences Listing and pinpointed his Greens, Yellows, and Reds during a seminar I was leading. During a break in the schedule, he came up to me with a knowing glint in his eye—almost like a kid caught with his hand in the cookie jar.

He said: "Dick, I know what I wish I was, and that is a Strategy person. But I know I am not that, I am a Relationships person." During this conference, we worked out a different job description for him, getting him out to be with customers more and doing more PR work, and less office work (which he assigned to someone else).

It took humility and maturity for him to reach this conclusion and make those changes. This is a perfect application of how the Green Light Concept can help a person make decisions with himself or herself in mind, which means he or she is more apt to lead a God-pleasing life. Facts from a Positive Experiences Listing are friendly. Today, Fred is a much happier business owner, husband, father, and churchgoer. He is being himself, his most genuine self. I believe God is pleased, too.

4. UNDERSTAND what the words Strategy, Tasks, Ideas, Relationships mean.

These word descriptions are not meant to pigeonhole people or label them. Instead, they represent broad areas so a person can get handles on whom they are and so help them clarify their life direction as they think through their situation.

All four words—Strategy, Tasks, Ideas, and Relationships are used in our everyday conversation. So a person may have a strategy for cleaning a building, or designing a product, or cooking a meal, or counseling someone, or preparing a sermon.

Because they use the word strategy in everyday conversation does not make them a Strategy person when viewed through the eyes of the Green Light Concept. Same goes for Ideas, or Tasks, or Relationships. So while we may all agree relationships are important, or talk about how important relationships are on the job or at home, it does not mean we are automatically Relationships people.

I hope these four guidelines help you reach accurate conclusions about your Strategy, Tasks, Ideas, and Relationships tendencies. Repeating: this information is to help you get handles on your skills and areas of satisfaction . . . nothing more, nothing less.

THE GREEN MAGNET WITHIN, REVISITED

In Chapter 2 we said that satisfaction acts like a magnet on our thoughts and actions, in that we are drawn (like paper clips to a magnet) to think about and do things (because of the way God created us) that we do well (use our Green skills) and give us a sense of accomplishment or satisfaction. In other words, our Greens usually exert a strong, if not powerful influence (Green magnet effect) on what we do and how we do things.

So Strategy's Green magnet sees him or her drawn towards competitive situations or doing things requiring him or her to be selling all the time. Similarly, Tasks Green Magnet sees him or her trying to do every step right, whether other people see it or not. Ideas Green magnet within sees him or her constantly using their creative and inventive Green skills to produce innovative end-products or make new discoveries. Relationships Green magnet often causes him or her to gravitate towards lots of people interaction and doing such things as always encouraging people and uplifting sagging spirits.

Each of these above examples may be overstatements and oversimplifications. But they do illustrate the Green tendencies inside each one of us. Of course, as responsible people, we should not let such tendencies go unchecked; often we have to temper our tendencies because a situation before us now may require us to adjust our Green inclinations. If we don't, the results could be disastrous.

So would you use your imagination in this illustration of how our Green Magnet within will operate (if left unchecked)? Here is the situation. After a picnic of 85 people, there are dirty dishes, pots and pans to wash (no paper plates are at this auspicious occasion nor is an automatic dishwasher available). Let us notice how S, T, I, and R will wash the dishes. No snickering, please!

> SUE STRATEGY. Step back! She attacks the job. She fills the sink to the brim with water, and puts too much soap in. She tries competing—rushing through the job, spilling water on floor and people. Results show. Many items still have barbecue sauce on them. She breaks seven water glasses but "only" five dinner plates. What a mess!

Recall Strategy's Green skills: directing a large organization, selling, competing, and speaking to large audiences. She does none of this while washing dishes. The job is a total Red for her.

TOM TASKS. Will approach the job methodically—do the water glasses first, saucers second, etc. He changes water every 10 minutes. While washing, he gets every speck off every item; he examines it before putting an item in the drying rack. He does the job carefully as if handling expensive dinnerware, rather than everyday dinnerware. It takes forever. The person taking him home waits two hours for him to finish.

Recall Task's Greens. They usually involve projects, e.g. washing dishes, and assuming washing/cleaning or shaping up/tidying up was something he did at least twice in his Positive Experiences, he will tend to do the job right, perfectly right. When he is done (all but his "ride home" person left hours ago), the dishes and entire kitchen area is spotless. Just before leaving he gave the area a once-over to double check and make sure everything was in order.

ISABELLE IDEAS. Finally, Ideas starts, only after propping a book in front of her to read while washing the dishes. She seems preoccupied, and she is. She is thinking about and pondering her next research project or design concept. She washes in a half-hearted, disinterested manner. She is bored stuff.

Recall Ideas Greens. Dishwashing requires no researching, designing, teaching, or performing. She neither discovers/learns nor produces an original design (or end-product). For Ideas, this is mindless work. The job is Red, very Red for her.

RONNIE RELATIONSHIPS. While washing dishes, Relationships keeps talking to people, far and near. His eyes wander through the kitchen spotting friends and striking up conversations . . . all the while he is washing dishes; at least some dishes get washed. With all the people around, he is having a high old time. The stacked dishes are an eyesore, stacked every which way (Tasks goes crazy seeing that!). "Got to think positive," he keeps saying.

Recall Relationships Greens. He receives satisfaction interacting with people, not dirty dishes. He is most effective visiting, socializing, greeting people, doing PR work, etc., not splashing around in soapy water and washing dishes.

Mini "Washing-the-dishes" Summary: I hope through these four outlandish, exaggerated illustrations you see in simplistic, yet realistic ways, how Strategy, Tasks, Ideas, and Relationships tend to function (their natural, unchecked tendencies), in turn, helping you discover, or understand better, your Greens and Reds.

CHAPTER SUMMARY

"I never looked at myself this way," Laura relates. "Frankly, I would have guessed I was a Relationships person, not an Ideas person. This is so insightful. And using Green, Yellow, and Red to get across the concept that people have areas of skills (Greens, so tend to 'go') and areas where they are not as skilled (Reds, so tend to 'drag their feet') makes so much sense. It helps me get a practical handle on things. I am glad I took the time to list my life's Positive Experiences."

You have just completed a very important exercise. It may not be as "thrilling" to do as winning a gold medal at the Olympics, scoring the winning goal, making the dean's list, or knitting a scarf. However, think of your Positive Experiences from God's standpoint. He wants you to be satisfied and use your skills, so He has engineered your life to have a series of Positive Experiences. Is this a blessing? I'd like to think so. Are Positive Experiences perhaps also special gifts from God, along with things like friends, church, family, etc.? I'd like to think so.

As road signs give valuable information and directions to motorists, so do Positive Experiences give valuable information (about Greens and Reds) and directions (what opportunities to be pursuing) to you and me. We will be talking Greens, Reds, and Positive Experiences throughout this book.

God is pleased when we walk closely with Him; He must be disappointed when we allow life to pull us away from Him. Green work enables people to have the potential for a close walk with Him; Red work has the opposite effect. And what is "Green with God?" To please Him, use our God-given Greens, and walk closely with Him.

CHAPTER 4
WHERE IS YOUR HEART?

The *goal* of this chapter is to examine our heart inclinations, so that as we are thinking through future decision options, we will do it with prepared hearts and focused-on-God minds. In so doing, we will be more apt to hear God's "still small voice" acting on our minds, wills, and emotions via the mysterious operation of His Holy Spirit.

INTRODUCTION

At this point, you should have a handle on your Greens, Yellows, and Reds (plus a copy of your Positive Experiences conveniently tucked away, but right at your fingertips). The process we used to discover them was comparatively straightforward and logical . . . a listing, then assessment of your listing to uncover your Greens and Reds.

Most people, believers or not, can list Positive Experiences and then discover their Greens and Reds. The Holy Spirit is always present in a believer helping and encouraging, but non-believers can also figure out their Greens and Reds on their own (without the Spirit's help).

But now we are going to turn a corner, and start thinking about the future. In so doing, we will be looking at less objective and logical areas. Without meaning to imply there are times we need God's Guiding/Helping Spirit and times we do not, we especially need the mind of God as we take steps to make sure our hearts are prepared to discern specifically what would be God-pleasing decisions.

So in this chapter, we will be dealing with the heart condition in terms of its receptivity to ingest God's Word and in this process, discern His Wishes and Desires. We will begin thinking about what it is we really want to do with our lives. These issues, along with others, require His Holy Spirit to encourage and counsel us. That is, if our main desire is to please Him, not ourselves.

With the help of the Holy Spirit, we can "set [y]our hearts on things above" (Colossians 3:1) as well as "set [y]our minds on things above" (Colossians 3:2). This will help us be more apt to look at things from God's viewpoint, rather than what the secular world or people may be telling us.

Paul, writing to Timothy in 2 Timothy 2:7, said. "Reflect on what I am saying, for the Lord will give you insight into all of this." My hope, in this process, is that the Lord will give you insight into how to best use your Greens and Reds for His Glory as you read and study His Word. Think of it: He has promised insight to us. Are we prepared to grasp His insights, then act on them?

OUR SPIRITUAL UMBRELLA: THE PSALM 37:4 PROMISE

If we want reassurance that God desires to imbue our thoughts, desires and goals, then Psalm 37:4 should encourage us to trust Him with all our hearts, souls, and might. You know what it says: "Delight yourself in the Lord and he will give you the desires of your heart." Who will? He will. And what will He give you? The desires of your heart. Is this a reckless promise by God, or one to be taken seriously by us? And does He really mean it?

I hate to admit this now, but for many years I misused this verse by virtually ignoring "Delight yourself in the Lord" and just claiming "He will give you the desires of your heart." You see, that sounded good to me . . . the desires of my heart. I wanted that.

But I really believe I missed the point because it all starts and ends with "Delight yourself in the Lord." Then I also mistakenly misinterpreted what the word "desires" meant. Again, I am so thankful we have an Advocate, Jesus, who gives us sinful, often careless people access to a Holy God (1 John 2:1): "But if anybody does sin, we have one who speaks to the Father in our defense—Jesus Christ, the Righteous One." With this in mind, let's see what Psalm 37:4 is really saying, then see how we can practically apply it.

"DELIGHT YOURSELF IN THE LORD"

What does "delight" mean? To delight means (from dictionary) to take pleasure in, to enjoy in and of itself. So a person may say: "I take great delight in driving my car" or "going to the beach" or "taking hikes" or "visiting relatives." The activity itself is pleasurable. Nothing else is needed to give enjoyment.

So if I delight in being with you, it means I like being with you, making it a pleasant time for me. As I spend more and more time with you, your ideas and thoughts will begin "sinking in" and most likely influence my thinking. I would respect you, trust you, and in my eyes, you have credibility. I simply enjoy being in your presence . . . and vice-versa (I hope!).

So to delight in the Lord means I enjoy being with God, that I trust Him without reservations, I like spending time with Him and calling on Him from time to time to say thanks or make a request. And as I study His Word and pray, His Thoughts begin "sinking in" influencing my thinking.

All said differently, He Himself is what I desire. "Whom have I in heaven but you? And earth has nothing I desire besides you" (Psalm 73:25). "Then I will go to the altar of God, to God, my joy and my delight" (Psalm 43:4).

In a nutshell, to delight in the Lord means I have full confidence in God, I value God, I revere Him; and I am experiencing NOW His Love and Goodness. No human or earthly desire should relegate God to second place; as Psalm 73:25 says that "earth has nothing" compared to what we have in God. No job, person, car, house, trip can ever compare to God. God Himself is our one and only passion.

This is the mindset that is foundational to His granting [us] the desires of [our] hearts (second part of Psalm 37:4). As such, we are more apt to "set [our] hearts and minds on things above," rather than on "earthly things" (Colossians 3:1, 2).

Unless my foremost desire is God himself, then my mind will allow all sorts of stuff to enter it, especially what I see—things and people. As a result, I lose God-consciousness; in effect, God gets relegated to second or third place. Instead, God wants our central focus to be Him and Him alone, period. AND He wants us to deepen our fellowship with Him; He never shuts the door, leaving us standing alone on the front steps. Plus we cannot love others (Universal Calling) unless God's love in us is our inspiration to reach out to others.

Do you think this perspective pleases God? You bet it does . . . AND it delights or pleases us because of the joy of God (God-confidence) that enriches our lives. Let's look now at the second part of Psalm 37:4.

"AND HE WILL GIVE YOU THE DESIRES OF YOUR HEARTS."

The context of this Psalm is righteous living . . . living "Christianly" (As we all know, the Bible is a book about righteous living; it is not a vocational handbook). So when we are delighting in the Lord, then He promises to give us the desires of our hearts, which pertain to living righteously and Christianly.

All said differently, the context of this Psalm is not primarily job-related, which is how I misused this Psalm. More about that in a moment. So as you use and apply this verse, you should be careful not to just ask yourself "Where is my heart?" or "What is it I desire in my heart to do (job-related)?", pray about it, and expect God to give it to you just like that. It is not that simple; there is a higher/different purpose behind this verse that needs to be addressed.

I do not recall where I read this quote which has helped me over the years: "To spiritualize your life, spiritualize your desires." That is another way to express the essence of Psalm 37:4.

So the desires of our hearts (Psalm 37:4) should be first and foremost those pertaining to our spiritual lives and result in righteous living. Let us call these *spiritual heart desires*. Other desires of my life such as for my job or family occur within the umbrella of desires for my spiritual life. See fig. 4-a.

fig. 4-a

In other words, just as our Individual Calling occurs within the umbrella (fig.1-c) of our Universal Calling, so our individual Job Heart Desires occur within (and greatly influenced by) the umbrella of our Spiritual Heart Desires.

I have misused this verse for many years by unintentionally ignoring the context of this Psalm—righteous living. I would simply say to myself and to others I was trying to help: "Where is your heart? What is it that you really want to do?" In so doing, first, I ignored the "Delight yourself in the Lord" concept. Second, I relegated, so misused, "He will give you the desires of your heart" by thinking of it mainly in a job context, rather than what it is . . . a spiritual context.

Our spiritual heart desires should supersede any and all other desires— urgent and critical as they may seem to us right now. Just step away for a second, and think of the wonderful, peace-giving promise: If we will delight in Him, then He will give us what we deeply, from-the-heart desire spiritually. Do you trust Him enough for THAT?

So when I surface my spiritual heart desires, this rises to the top: to please God, to live Christianly, to walk closer to Him, and keep on trying to see other people through the eyes of Jesus (this is a real struggle for me).

In my opinion, spiritual heart desires tend to be individual, so my desires may ring hollow with you. So you might come up with things like: to live a holy life (1 Peter 1:15), or trust God more (John 14:1), or bring every thought captive/obedient to Him (2 Corinthians 10:5), or be a more consistent prayer (Ephesians. 5:18), or to spend more time studying/meditating on Scripture ". . . on his law he meditates day and night" (Psalm1:2), and so on.

Another person might express his or her spiritual heart desires as to love God wholeheartedly (Matthew 22:37), or to be faithful (Hebrews 11:6), or to be a kingdom principled and living person (Matthew 6:33), and so on.

Desires are important. Most people agree that desires impact our beliefs and values, our attitudes, and then our behavior. The question is: "Are you delighting in God? Are you deadly serious about living for Him? Are you embracing (and so living out) spiritual desires"?

If we are delighting in the Lord, then His Promise to us individually is . . . He will *give* (not charge or bill us) us the desires of our hearts.

What is one result? You will not be able to "hide your light under a bowl" (Matthew 5:15). People will see and notice. "When they . . . realized that they were . . . ordinary men . . . they took note that these men had been with Jesus" (Acts 4:13). Our "light" and witness is not a conscious experience. God is at work in your life. But others both see and experience His Love and Work in you . . . yes even through ordinary people like you and me. Trust God, not your experience or how you feel at the moment. God will work in spite of how we feel. *Thank you, Lord for that.*

In a nutshell, a person's spiritual heart desires are the tail that wags the dog, when it comes to "Where is your heart" issues. They keep our minds focused on God and spiritual issues. The heart is central. Is your heart in being Christian, or isn't it? You and I must not waffle over this issue.

In the Bible, especially the Old Testament, heart often means the point of divine contact with mankind. The word "heart" usually means "all my being"—mind, emotions, and will. God's contact with us is in our minds, as well as emotions and will. Do we want God to speak to us? Please think carefully about this question and what it might mean or cost . . . before saying a quick "yes" or "why of course." And if yes, what is one way we can cooperate with God to accomplish this?

WHERE IS YOUR JOB HEART?

As we just saw, our Spiritual Heart Desires are paramount. They form an umbrella within which we can develop job possibilities we trust will be God-pleasing. Now, within that umbrella, we can ask: "Where is my heart? If I could do what I really wanted to do, what would I do?"

People will tend to do things that interest them . . . or pursue things that concern them. They will usually take the initiative to do things they desire doing, what their hearts are into—whether that is to write, bake, clean, fabricate, research, fix, speak, or whatever. And if a person can do things that can capitalize on his or her knowledge strengths, it is both confidence-building and education-verifying.

Look at Fig. 4-b. This Job Decision Checklist contains a suggested decision process for figuring out your life direction. There is one piece missing—Life Purpose, which we will consider in the next chapter.

JOB DECISION CHECKLIST
(Full-time work)

Use this Checklist as follow-up to discovering your Greens and Reds. While information about Greens and Reds is foundational, other areas listed below also play an important role in your decision process.

A   l ist your...

1.   INTERESTS AND CONCERNS. Look at your whole life—work, volunteer activities, hobbies, leisure time, etc., not just one area of your life like work or hobbies. What interests you? What needs, problems, issues concern you?

2.   DESIRES AND ASPIRATIONS. If you could do what you really wanted, what would you do? Where is your heart? When you are alone—thinking, fantasizing—what do you see yourself doing?

3.   KNOWLEDGE STRENGTHS. These are things you know fairly well. Look back over all your experiences—educational, work, volunteer, leisure activities, etc. As you do this, don't compare yourself with other people.

B.   MATCH-UP. Match-up is how well each item you listed (A 1, 2, and 3) is compatible with your Greens and what you did in your Positive Experiences. If an item matches up a lot, mark it G (Green); if it matches up some, mark it Y (Yellow); if it matches up very little, mark it R (Red).

If an item seems more personal values/priorities-related, mark it V for values. If an item seems more hobbies-related, mark it A for avocation. Or if an item is Difficult To Classify, mark it DTC.

fig. 4-b

C. JOB OPTION possibilities. In light of the above information, list some specific jobs or potential job opportunities that would best utilize your Greens, and capitalize on your knowledge strengths or other past experiences. Remember your GOAL is to HEAD IN A GREEN DIRECTION; or, said differently, to avoid or minimize using your Reds a lot. You should list at least two job options, or a couple more if you can.

D. SEARCH OUT the field, business or industry that would represent places to look for and/or find a Green-for-you job. Talk to people in that field, business, or industry, asking for their help/advice. Research other resources—books, Internet, etc. Talk to anyone who might know something about the field, business or industry (networking).

E. JOB MATCH-UP. Always find out the three or four key/priority responsibilities for a job. Then do a Green, Yellow, Red Job Match-up with each of those responsibilities.

Finally, ask yourself: Will this job enable me to realize my Individual Calling? Will the job enable me to use my Greens and some of my Reds, realize my (or our) Values and Priorities, and achieve my Life Purpose/Goals? Will it please God?

fig. 4-b(2)

INTERESTS & CONCERNS: Right now, look only at A, items 1, 2, and 3. Take time now to jot down a few things that come to mind. There are no right or wrong answers. When I did this twenty years ago, I listed the following for A: 1: high schoolers; college students; people having job problems; floundering churches; misled people; mistreated and poor people; helping someone do well spiritually; helping organizations develop their employees.

Another person's listing may be totally different. It may include items like: abortion; political corruption; the unsaved; mathematics; missions; architecture; and the like.

Or someone may list items like: photography; art; the environment; people who drop out of the church; family; elderly parents, unethical business practices; woodworking; etc.

Here is the point. Do some brainstorming as you do this. Let your mind hit the paper. Do not analyze and re-analyze what you write . . . just write down your thoughts. As we will do for each of the three (A, 1, 2, 3), we will evaluate each one by deciding how well each item is compatible with your Greens and what you wrote in your Positive Experiences Listing. See fig. 4-b, item B, Match-up. As an aside, I hope you are really seeing how important it is to at least list your Positive Experiences; they are a key information resource and decision sounding board.

Our goal is for a person to be heading in a Green direction, and to avoid or minimize going in a Red direction. Please read this next sentence carefully. For some reason, people list things in items A 1, 2, and 3 that not only lie within in their Greens, but also outside their Greens, so are in their Yellows and Reds.

A huge mistake people make is pursuing an Interest, only to find out later that that job or Interest did not use their Greens. In other words, they landed smack in the middle of their Reds. That is ugly. And most likely they had no idea or concept of Greens and Reds.

At this point, I am not saying not to do a Red, but my point is: a person needs to do enough Green "stuff" to receive Job Satisfaction (Ecclesiastes 5:18-20). How you handle Reds is your decision. But do not let Reds dominate.

So to avoid this happening, I strongly advise people to do the Match-up exercise. Virtually everyone I help through this process will list items that do not match up well with their Greens.

So when I did the Match-up exercise for my Interests and Concerns, two items turned out Red—high schoolers, and mistreated/poor people. I did nothing like this in my Positive Experiences. Could I include them in my Service-to-Others life? Yes, but I should do this knowing in advance it is a Red. More about that in Chapter 7.

DESIRES & ASPIRATIONS: Now go to item A. 2, Desires and Aspirations. This is the big one! Do not rush doing it. Do not be unduly influenced by other people. Remember, it is you, not them, who must be doing the work day-in, day-out. Only you know your Job Heart Desires. You may list just one item, or three items, or whatever.

So ask yourself: Where is my heart? If I could do what you really wanted to do, what would I do or be doing? Write down what comes to mind.

When I asked myself this question three years before starting my present business, I answered this way: My heart was in having my own business, working it out of our home, throwing out every business practice that did not jive with my Christian beliefs/principles, and not growing (growing into a large business; in other words, staying small).

My heart aspirations are the same today, 30 years later. I am doing essentially the same things now as when I started. The essence of my business is consulting (along with some training) about organizational issues, selection of people, solving people problems, and career planning.

Heart aspirations are individual. So most likely the last two paragraphs mean nothing to you. Your heart aspirations will be yours, mine will be mine.

Some people's heart aspirations may change from time to time. However, what tends not to change is what gives them Job Satisfaction and their Skills. So their change is really in using their Greens and some of their Reds in a different setting or with different people.

Generalizing now, a person's heart aspirations usually reflect his or her Greens and also his or her Positive Experiences. So a Strategy person with competing Skills may have as a heart aspiration to coach a team to a division title. A Strategy person with convincing Skills may have as a heart aspiration to convince people to buy product X.

An Ideas person with writing Skills may have as a heart aspiration to write a book on subject X that adds value to people's family life or work life.

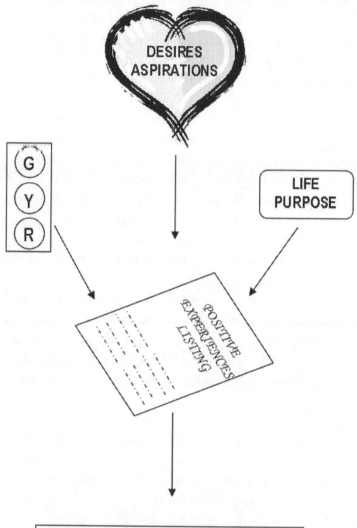

fig. 4-c

A Tasks person with cleaning/refurbishing or painting Skills may have as a heart aspiration to start a business, grow it to 25 people, and provide appropriate refurbishing services to both businesses and residences.

In a nutshell and oversimplifying, our job heart aspirations usually include both what gives us satisfaction and what will best utilize our skills. So look at your Positive Experiences and use them as an information resource. See fig. 4-c.

Think about, study, and reflect on what you did in your Positive Experiences. Do not dismiss them as "has-beens" or just past events. They are loaded with information you developed, so it is accurate and reliable.

So a Relationships person's head and heart will tend to be in Relationships-related issues. So if, for example, his or her Skills include doing PR work, building relationships, and organizing and coordinating special events, then his or her heart desires/aspirations should reflect that.

You may come up with two to four "Where is your heart?" possibilities. Then use your Positive Experiences Listing and Greens as decision sounding boards. Do the Match-up exercise, Item B, fig. 4-b. Ask yourself: "Which of them will best utilize or maximize my Greens? Least utilize my Greens? Could one or two possibilities be combined?" Things may be still fuzzy for you; that is fine. Rome was not built in a day.

What all this means is your job heart aspirations will and should point you in a Green direction—that is, enable you to use your Greens. Is it God-pleasing to use what He wired us to do? Yes.

Time is not the issue when coming up with your heart aspirations. It may take you two hours or two months (or longer) to formulate your heart aspirations. Fine. It is well worth the time. Scripture is very clear about having our hearts in what we do. ". . . Work at it with all your heart" (Colossians 3:23).

All things being equal, we human beings will be most apt to work at it with all our hearts when the core of what we do uses our Greens (Isn't Scripture practical!). A reminder: we are talking about time-consuming, ongoing responsibilities, not once-a-month or five-minute projects. So when our hearts are in what we do every day, we will tend to work hard at it, diligently and conscientiously, and find the work meaningful to us.

People get little or no satisfaction doing something half-heartedly or with no umph or excitement. Your heart is in what you do, or it is not.

Scripture (Colossians 3:23) is clear as a bell; we are to work at it whole-heartedly—"with <u>all</u> your heart." It cannot be faked, for very long at least. Your Positive Experiences Listing is loaded with many "all your heart" possibilities.

KNOWLEDGE STRENGTHS. Then go to item A, 3, fig.4-b, Knowledge Strengths. List things you know fairly well. When I did this while figuring out my life direction, I listed the following: leadership research, the essentials of supervision; training principles; selection/screening principles; how people learn.

The purpose for listing Knowledge Strengths is to capitalize on them in a job search, job decision process. Of course, if your Job Heart Desires lie outside your Knowledge Strengths, then most likely further training and education is required.

So list your Knowledge Strengths. This is neither a horn-tooting exercise nor an exercise to point out how little you know. It is simply an exercise to surface an area of your strengths that is good to know in a job decision process. Then do the Match-up exercise, item B, fig. 4-b.

Most likely your three lists—Interests and Concerns, Job Heart Desires and Aspirations, and Knowledge Strengths exist only in your mind, or perhaps you jotted a few things down on a piece of paper. In either case, take the time to put your thoughts on paper now while you are thinking along these terms.

We are going to switch gears for a moment. As we have been thinking and writing things down, we are believing and hoping that our thoughts reflect His Thoughts, that our desires reflect His Desires for our lives. This is a big step of faith to believe this and trust God this way. But this is what He has instructed us to do. And without meaning to sound presumptuous, let us see how God's Spirit may be impacting your thought process. I call this the "Bubble Up" Concept and "Sprinkle Down" Concept. I hope these two very simple concepts will encourage you.

THE BUBBLE UP CONCEPT

Most people have down deep inner stirrings that often represent what they would really like to do. The questions *Where is your heart? What is it that you would really like to do? What gets you heart beating a bit faster/ excitedly?* are designed to surface/express a person's job heart desires.

If this is a fairly strong from-the-heart desire, and a person tries to dismiss it or forget it, it usually re-emerges, bubbles up again. So a person may say, "I just can't get this off my mind" or "I have always had this inner urge to do X." In my view, such repeated bubble ups need expression, and after appropriate thinking about whether such an aspiration uses our Greens or not, properly and sanely implemented.

Terry, in his late 40s, is in a Red job (Red meaning uses mainly his Reds, rather than his Greens). He said: "I have always had this yearning . . . it keeps coming AND coming back (he was so emphatic about it). I sometimes feel I am ready to blow up." Terry was in a high-paying job, prestigious too, judging by the living standards of his friends. They thought he was success personified.

But Terry's *heart* was not in his work. What kept coming back *(bubbling up)* was this yearning to be an advertising designer. So he called me for my opinion. A review of his Greens and Positive Experiences revealed such work would land him smack in the middle of his Greens.

Over an 18-month period, he and his wife redirected their lifestyle and life priorities. Now he says: "I am excited about going to work . . . I no longer get tense Sunday afternoons thinking about the week ahead . . . now I can't wait to get to work."

Did Terry make a God-pleasing decision? I believe so. God wants us to responsibly use the Greens He gave us. Not too incidentally, Terry is also getting back on track about spending time alone with God each day, studying his Bible and praying as never before. "I have never been so close to God," he shared. And he said this with a thankful heart. It all started with this "yearning" in His heart. God, the Initiator, is quietly at work!

In my mid- to late-20s, I had this inner urge to get into training and education. This desire would not go away; it kept bubbling up. My sales manager at the time laughed it off, saying, "There's no money in that end of things."

A year later, I took action. I resigned my position and headed off into the unknown world of training. I never regretted the decision. I still have training/education-related desires—they keep bubbling up. My latest is to do seminars/workshops for people around the theme: "Abiding in Christ" or around the theme: "What is Green with God?" I get excited thinking about it . . . but not excited about marketing (my Red) it!!!

THE SPRINKLE DOWN CONCEPT

The Sprinkle Down Concept refers to God's Holy Spirit "Sprinkling Down" into our thoughts, ideas, and desires; and into our hearts, the point of God's Divine Contact with us. In so doing, He influences us in incomprehensible and experiential ways, so what bubbles up is most apt to be God-pleasing desires.

As believers, we know the Holy Spirit takes residence in us when we receive Jesus as Savior.

However, in this thinking, brainstorming, creative process of coming up with our spiritual heart desires and job heart desires, I believe we still should do two things. One, ask for the Holy Spirit (Luke 11:13) and two, ask for wisdom (James 1:5; 3:17).

Then by faith ("without faith it is impossible to please God"—Hebrews 11:6) we trust God (John 14:1) that His Holy Spirit sprinkled and penetrated our thoughts. Pushing this point even more, we trust that He initiated such spiritual and job heart desires, so what bubbles up are most likely God-pleasing ideas. How this in fact happens in detail is a mystery. So by faith we reach up to God; with faith, we take seriously the heart stirrings/desires HE creates in us.

Said differently, God's suggestions come to us in the form of heart desires that spring up from within us so that we tend to want to obey willingly (the Green Magnet within) and from a grateful heart. This is a world apart from ideas that come to us as directives from the outside that we robustly obey (often unwillingly), but we do because we are good troopers.

In a nutshell, a person usually wants to do what his or her heart is telling him or her to do rather than doing something "dragging their heels" because their heart is not in it.

I truly hope the "Bubble Up" and "Sprinkle Down" Concepts will fuel your desires and renew your "delight in the LORD" (Ps. 37:4).

REGULATORS

We began this chapter by saying God has promised to give us the spiritual desires of our hearts (Ps. 37:4). They act as an umbrella under which we think through and list our Interests and Concerns, Desires and Aspirations, and Knowledge Strengths. Expressed differently, our *spiritual heart desires* act as regulators in that they keep us focused in a spiritual direction. Without these regulators, a person is apt to portray as spiritual the desires and goals that look good, sound good, impress people, but are really designed to make him or her look successful in the eyes of the world.

Spiritual heart desires remind us of our sinful nature, the need for a pure-before-God heart ("Blessed are the pure in heart"—Matthew 5:8), and that He sees and knows our heart motives. They remind us we are here to glorify and serve Him, and Him alone.

CHECKING THINGS OUT

Even though we have done our best at surfacing job heart desires within the umbrella of our spiritual heart desires, yet we know our heart can do things that baffle us. The prophet Jeremiah wrote (17:9): "The heart is deceitful above all things and beyond cure. Who can understand it?"

Because the heart is so critical in this process, I suggest a person periodically examine his or her "heart condition" and "heart receptivity," which I believe are God-pleasing things to do.

EXAMINE YOUR HEART CONDITION. Are your motives pure? Or is there some sin that needs to be confessed that you know via His Holy Spirit's prompting that you should take care of now, removing known impurities so you can have as pure a heart before God as possible? Known sin will most likely block your hearing God's still small voice during the Sprinkle Down, Bubble Up process. God knows and sees your heart. God is on your side. He wants what is best for you. Selfish motives, unhealthy desires, self-serving initiatives usually mean "dry spells" spiritually.

EXAMINE YOUR HEART RECEPTIVITY. Besides motives, another aspect of our heart condition is its *receptivity* to God's Word. In that sense, do you have a receptive heart? Remember the parable of the sower. The seed, God's Word, often falls on deaf ears—hard, impenetrable soil—hard, impenetrable hearts, but good soil is receptive. Those represented by the good soil "hear the word, accept it, and produce . . ." (Mark 4:20). James 1:21b instructs us: "Humbly accept the word planted in you . . . ." The word "accept" appears in both verses; it has the connotation of a soft heart or receptive heart (receptive soil). God's Word is accepted by a soft receptive heart.

Is your heart in a receptive condition? When you read Scripture, does it sink in? Are you ready to "humbly accept the word planted"? (James 1:21b) Is Scripture a first love in your life? God does speak through His Word and as we think and meditate on it, thoughts bubble up as His Holy Spirit does His work.

Do you really want God to speak to you? Have you asked Him lately to speak to you with words like: "Lord, I want to do what would please You. Please speak to me—my mind and heart are open to You. What is it You desire?"

In a nutshell, your response in cooperation with God's Spirit working on your mind and in your heart should be YOUR individual thoughts and ideas. At this juncture, do not be unduly influenced by what you read others are doing or what a mentor/friend says. This is your life being lived before God; it is you who has to do the "toilsome work" (Ecclesiastes 5:18). Advice, while appreciated, is just that, advice. It is you who must produce day-in, day-out.

So while CHECKING THINGS OUT because our hearts (with Satan's help) have the potential to deceive us, we should do at least two things: Examine our heart condition and heart receptivity so we are more apt to hear His still small Voice through the noise and clutter that surrounds us.

BACK TO THE JOB DECISION CHECKLIST

Look again at the Job Decision Checklist, fig. 4-b. Item C is JOB OPTION possibilities. I am suggesting is that you list specific job or potential job opportunities that would best utilize your Greens and capitalize on your Knowledge Strengths. Further, Item D suggests SEARCHING OUT fields, businesses, or industries that would represent places to look for and/or find a Green-for-you job. We will take up item E. Job Match-up in the next chapter.

DRAWING A BLANK. Occasionally a person may have a hard time (for any number of reasons) thinking up specific job or field possibilities. He or she may be discouraged, beaten down, emotionally drained, hurt by fractured relationships, and the like. So it is hard for him or her to come up with something specific and concrete.

When this happens, I suggest two things to people.

1. Pray about it. Ask God to restore your spirits and energize your mind.
2. Spend some more time going over your Positive Experiences Listing. They are a gold mine of information. As you do this, ask yourself:
    a. Is there one of them that contains the core of what I really want to be doing?
    b. Is there a way to combine two or three of them into a job possibility?
    c. Which two, three, or four Positive Experiences represent what I really want to do?

LIVING BY THE SPIRIT

As we have just read, our hearts are deceitful (Jeremiah 19:9), so we have to keep examining our heart condition? And if that is not enough, our human nature also raises its ugly head with its selfish ambitions, jealousy, and the like (Galatians 5:19-21). A double salvo: "Enough already," you are saying.

But we have this promise of all promises: "Live by the Spirit, and you will not gratify the desires of the sinful nature." (Galatians 5:16) This verse has profound meaning in living out our calling as well as figuring out our spiritual and job heart aspirations. In a nutshell and oversimplifying, to live by the Spirit means to live our life by, around, and through the Holy Spirit; and to walk intimately with God, that is, in close touch with God.

So if a person is making his or her best effort to do that (often stubbing their toes in the process), then God promises he or she will not gratify (live out) the desires of their sinful nature.

I would rather stake my claim on that promise, rather than the promise of any human being— spoken or written. PLEASING GOD AND LIVING OUT OUR CALLING IS A SPIRITUAL PROCESS AT EVERY TURN.

SUMMARIZING

We have been seeing through the instruction of Psalm 37:4, that if we are delighting in the Lord, then He will give us the desires of our hearts. These desires are "righteous living" in nature, not job or job position they are in nature.

That being the case, then in thinking through our Job heart desires, we trust that God will sprinkle down His Holy Spirit and imbue our ideas/ thoughts. Then what bubbles up is most apt to be God-pleasing and God-glorifying—things we can do wholeheartedly, rather than half-heartedly. God's confirmation will be His Peace you sense in your heart.

Proverbs 4:23 tells us: "Above all else, guard your heart, for it is the wellspring of life." Guarding our hearts should be one of our priorities. How? One way to guard it is with daily intake of His Word. Watch over it by asking His Holy Spirit to point out impurities that corrupt your motives. God welcomes your coming to Him. "Come to me [Jesus] . . ." Matthew 11:28.

> "Come near to God and he will come near to you. Wash your hands . . . purify your hearts . . . grieve, mourn, and wail . . . humble yourselves before the Lord, and he will lift you up"
>
> James 4:8-10.

He will lift you up and inspire you with hope, ideas, and peace. Your future is unknown, as is mine. What you and I do know, however, is that God is able and is working in you right now, period. Will you let Him do His Thing in your life? Who knows what Green possibilities may bubble up today or tomorrow or next week?

P.S. Perhaps you are asking: "Suppose a person is not a believer; can they have Job heart desires?" I believe they can and do have Job heart desires.

However, because his or her heart is not right with God, he or she does not have the benefit of His Holy Spirit in his or her thought processes. However, God may decide for reasons known only to Him to impose His Will on his or her decisions. God should not and cannot be programmed. God is God. We are finite human beings.

CHAPTER 5
LIVING RESPONSIBLY AMID LIFE'S REALITIES

"Live life, then, with a due sense of responsibility, not as men who do not know the meaning and purpose of life but as those who do." Ephesians 5:15 (Phillips)

The *goal* of this chapter is to show you how to evaluate a job or job opportunity in light of your Greens and Reds, personal Values-Priorities, and Life Purpose-Goals. You may recognize these three interrelated items as the three parts of the Individual Calling process described in Chapters 1 and 2. We will take up each of these three items separately in this chapter.

This means on the Individual Calling process illustration (fig. 1-b), the little hand will first be at the three o'clock (Greens and Reds) position, then six o'clock (Values-Priorities) and lastly nine o'clock (Life Purpose-Goals) positions. The big hand, as always, points upward to God.

INTRODUCTION

Recall that our Individual Calling process includes three interrelated parts. One, to <u>use</u> our God-given Greens and some of our God-given Reds; two, to <u>realize</u> our Values-Priorities; and three, to <u>achieve</u> our Life Purpose and Goals. In real life, we "work out" or actively use these three parts in order to be living a God-pleasing life.

To use, realize, and achieve (last paragraph), we must both understand what terms mean (e.g. Values-Priorities) and know how to use them. And to do this, our approach will be to:

1. Understand what **Job Match-up** means . . . in the process of <u>using</u> our God-given Greens and Reds. Job Match-up is how well the priority job responsibilities match up with or uses a person's Greens. A Green job uses his or her Greens a lot, and only some Red. A Yellow job uses some (not enough) Greens and quite a few Reds. A Red job uses mostly Reds, few if any Greens.

2. **Identify** or **Clarify** your Values-Priorities so that in your decision process, you can evaluate whether or not a particular job will enable you to <u>realize</u> your Values and Priorities. Some people say Values, others say Priorities. Either way, they represent what is really important to a person, married couple, family, and the like.

3. **Clarify** your Life Purpose and Goals to determine if a job will enable you to <u>achieve</u> your Life Purpose and Goals. Life Purpose represents the person or persons someone genuinely desires helping. Since we spend so much of our time on the job, it makes sense that our jobs enable us too achieve our Life Purpose. The appropriate Green job should do just that.

In each case, we are comparing the job with you, you meaning (1) your Greens, (2) your Values-Priorities, and (3) your Life Purpose. And depending on your situation, it may not be a "your" decision alone, but an "our" decision involving significant others in your life. In a moment we will consider each one more fully. First, a reality check.

OH, IF LIFE WOULD NOT GET SO COMPLICATED

As you look at and think about these three areas, I am sure you wish, as I do, that Living Out Our Calling was just one dimensional, rather than what it is, multi-dimensional. So instead of having to simultaneously consider three areas, have just one to "worry" about (Oh, if life itself were only simpler!). Frankly, many people do just that, only worry about Job, and often bypass thinking through their Values or considering their Life

Purpose. Usually there are harsh consequences that result, especially in lost or fractured relationships.

Gary, in his late 40's, traveled extensively in his job for a para-church organization whose main mission was worldwide evangelism. No one could question his "first love" and motives. He loved propagating the Gospel Message. As he poured out his heart to me, he said tearfully: "Dick, last week my daughter said to me, 'Dad, don't bother to come to my college graduation; you never came to anything else I did'."

Three months later he resigned from his position. Too late? I do not know. Did he make the right decision to resign? I do not know. What I do know is that he regretted his traveling life and the impact it had on his daughter. But I know it was right for him to go back to the drawing board and reshape his values, life purpose, and the like. He has a lot of bridges (relationships) to repair.

There are many "Gary-like" stories in the world touching all kinds of people in businesses, churches, community organizations, and more. We can be "married" to a hobby, or church, or a job, or educational program, or physical exercise program (all, I might add, for what appear to be logical reasons). That is, we can be married to one of these to the exclusion of other potential Values-Priorities like family, or spouse, or kids, helping needy people, etc.

So while it appears simpler (and it is) to consider only Job, or only Values, and the like, it is totally unrealistic. Because something is simple does not make it truth. The truth is life is complicated. In this case, the truth is we must live among life's ups and downs, victories and defeats, births and deaths, the seen and unseen, etc. But within these realities, we must remember our calling is to God, and a God-pleasing life.

So to help us gain perspective on our calling and begin understanding that, for most people a balanced life is at best a very wobbly balance, we will look briefly into two subjects: one, life's realities (that is, where we live) and two, what Scripture teaches.

1. Life's Realities

Life is complex, not simple . . . multi-dimensional, not singularly dimensional. To top that off, life is hard, not easy; often confusing and perplexing, rather than orderly and predictable. This is reality, the way it is, like it or not, for everyone, believers included.

Life happens. Our children act up in school. Cars break down. Traffic lights turn red when we are in a hurry or late. People lose jobs at the wrong time. Investments go up AND down. A spouse suddenly up and leaves their family. Droughts or floods ruin crops. Relationships break down; people fight. Tests reveal cancer. Love turns to hate. A tooth decides to ache just before an important business trip. God-fearing saints die prematurely. Thugs live a long life. A phone call could spell shock or joy. Fingers get caught in car doors. Trees fall on houses. Fire destroys; floods devastate. Your best intentioned, comprehensive plan for your life, month, or day can prevent none of these. We are all participants, like it or not.

2. Thank you, Lord, for Scripture

The realities of life cause me to look to Scripture, not to feed negative/discouraging thoughts but to gain perspective and so not overlook the good and Who is really in charge. Ecclesiastes feeds my soul: "When times are good, be happy; but when times are bad, consider: God has made the one as well as the other. Therefore, a man cannot discover anything about his future" Ecclesiastes 7:14.

Raw reality from Scripture tells us there are good times and bad times. And to top it all off, none of us knows or understands what is around the corner (our future). Then in chapter 9 and verse 1, the writer of Ecclesiastes writes: "So I reflected on all this and concluded that the righteous and the wise and what they do are in God's hands, but no man knows whether love or hate awaits him."

What this seems to be saying is that the scales of justice are not tipped in favor of a believer. Life delivers many unknowns, both good and bad, to everyone. However, if a person is trusting God and walking closely to Him, He gives that person a perspective and outlook that is an enabling force amidst life's ups and downs (or uncertainties).

So if something similar (e.g. tragedy or loss) happens to a believer and to a far-from-God non-believer, his or her reaction is different. If what happens is seen as from the hand of God (Ecclesiastes 9:1), the negative event can develop character in the believer, but most likely have little or no positive effect on the non-believer because they do not see things through

God's eyes. Similarly, opposite reactions if something good happens. A believer should be genuinely thankful to God, so receive the good happening gratefully and "ooze" with humility; a far-from-God non-believer reacts very differently, taking full credit for what happened, even bordering on arrogance and pride; God never enters into his or her thinking.

There is a lot, a whole lot, we do not understand. "As you do not know the path of the wind, or how the body is formed in a mother's womb, so you cannot understand the work of God, the maker of all things" Ecclesiastes 11:5. Scripture does not tell us to understand God or what He is doing; it tells us the opposite—that we cannot understand. So my understanding of life's realities is limited, very limited. Ecclesiastes 11:5 tells us we cannot understand the work of God. I accept that.

So our approach to life and our calling must take our lack of understanding into account fully. In the light of this, two choices await us. One, we can wring our hands, and take the attitude to do nothing or let it happen or just do it. Or two, we can take the attitude and belief that God gave us minds to use, emotions to feel, wills to exercise, a faith to exercise in a caring, loving, and sovereign God. We will choose the latter course of action, not the first. To do otherwise would be irresponsible.

I love Philippians 4:8: "Whatever is true . . . right . . . pure . . . lovely . . . admirable—if anything is excellent or praiseworthy—*think* about such things" (Emphasis added). What beautiful words—true, right, pure, lovely, etc. We are to *think* of such things and make decisions on what we do know, especially from Scripture, and do that God-confidently and trustingly. And that is what we are going to do . . . think about the rightness of a Green, satisfying job; the beauty of a God-pleasing definition of YOUR success; the excellence of having a life purpose that counts, in God's eyes.

You see, if we do not clarify things for us as God has directed our hearts and minds, we will simply get caught up in stuff and things, usually living "out of control" lifestyles which I do not think pleases God in the long run. Listen to Phillips translation of Romans 12:2: "Don't let the world around you squeeze you into its own mold, but let God re-mold your minds from within . . . ."

In a different context, yet I think it can apply here, Ecclesiastes 7:16-18 says: "Do not be overrighteous, neither be overwise . . . do not be over-wicked, and do not be a fool . . . the man who fears God will avoid all extremes."

"Avoid all extremes"—like being married to the one thing (as described earlier). What is one way to avoid extremes? By consciously thinking through each of the three areas so foundational to our calling. Repeating: this may at first blush sound complicated, but not nearly as complicated compared to the "un-thought-through" life and lifestyle.

By doing this (taking three areas rather than one into account), I believe we are taking a giant step towards avoiding the extreme of devoting ourselves ONLY or excessively to our job, or our hobby, etc. to the exclusion of other things important in life. In other words, bringing some semblance of balance and order into our overall lifestyle, life priorities, and the like (notice I did not say simply balance and order, but qualified it with "some semblance"—a balanced lifestyle is unattainable, which is OK since we do not know what is around the corner). We do this, knowing only God understands fully.

So the real question is: Do you believe God understands you and your circumstances? Do you know that what you know is shallow and incomplete, compared to what God knows? Most importantly, are you trusting Him, really trusting Him?

Let's do a mini-summary, using this quote from Oswald Chambers (Daily Thoughts for Disciples, pg. 227-228, Christian Literature Crusade):

> . . . We cannot do what God does and . . . God will not do what we can do. We cannot save ourselves or sanctify ourselves; God only can do that; but God does not give us good habits, He does not give us character, He does not make us walk aright; we must do all that. We have to work out what God has worked in (Philippians 2:12-13).

God will not do an "agenda drop" from the sky and tell you what your priorities and values should be. You must develop those . . . in light of Scripture. God is not going to write out or jot down your Greens and Reds on page 2 of the agenda drop; that is up to you and me to do for ourselves.

So because of Life's Realities and Scripture's teaching, it behooves you to ". . . make every effort to add to your faith . . ." (2 Peter 1:5) and to

1. Understand what Job Match-up means,
2. Identify your Values-Priorities, and
3. Clarify your Life Purpose.

Let's start doing that now.

1. UNDERSTAND WHAT JOB MATCH-UP MEANS

We have already touched on the Match-up concept in Chapter 4 and in the Job Decision Checklist, fig. 4-b. Let's continue that discussion.

Job Match-up is how well the priorities of a job match up, or uses, a person's Greens. The goal of Job Match-up is to enable a person to be effective (do well, A or B+ work), productive (achieve the goals/results at hand), and be satisfied (Ecclesiastes 5:18). In this process, we will be fitting the job to the person (Strengths-Greens), not vice versa—fitting the person to the job.

Let's illustrate this "fitting the person to the job" concept with this actual example, and I have had many like it over the years. Phillip Mack, thirty-two years old, graduated from college with honors. He seemed destined for success—"one who can't miss," as we would say.

Ten years later, he is a failure by all standards. He has succeeded at few things; in three different jobs he failed miserably. His frustrated and concerned supervisor said, "No one wants to hire him now . . . and I don't know what to do with him."

Together, Phillip and I pinpointed his Greens, Yellows, and Reds (Chapter 3), then compared them with his key responsibilities in his three jobs. What a revelation! Phillip was not using his Greens on the jobs. In other words, there was little match-up between Phillip's Greens and what he was expected to do. In all three jobs, he was in a Red job, not a Green job. Phillip's sense of worth was low because his sense of competence and accomplishment on his jobs was nil. He felt guilty and was told bluntly: "Phillip, you are a failure. You have no successes."

In one sense that was true; he had failed. In another sense, it was false, because Phillip himself did not fail. "*You* are not a failure, Phillip," I said. "The failure occurred in the match-up of your Greens and responsibilities." So-called constructive criticism from his supervisor, though well-intentioned, was like pounding him further into the ground. All he heard was negative things. Using this world's standards, he *was* a failure.

We chatted by his car as he was leaving. He said, "Are you saying *I am* not a failure?" I said "yes." A huge burden seemed to lift from his shoulders then and there.

This illustration has a positive ending. Prayer teams were set up for him. Four months later, a supervisor rejecting many business "success" standards hired Phillip. Basing the decision on matching the job to Phillip's Greens made sense to the supervisor. Now four years later, his supervisor is saying, "I have learned the fallacy of writing a job description without taking a person's Greens into account. Today my philosophy is 'Fit the job to the person, not the person to the job'." *Amen, I said to myself.*

Out there in the "wide world," you may be told the job description, but little effort is usually made to pinpoint your Greens. So it is literally up to you to do this Match-up exercise in light of the job under consideration.

Erika, using the Green discovery process in Chapter 3, pinpointed her Greens, Yellows, and Reds three years ago. She decided to stay living in her community, rather than move when her company was bought out by another company. So she had to find a new job.

She sent me the job description of a position that was attractive to her. Then as she studied it, and matched up the job to her Greens she said: "This job is setting me up for failure." What she meant was, the job did not use her Greens. In other words, she would have been heading in a Red direction—into a Red job.

To help people in this Job match-up process, I have prepared a Job Match-up Worksheet, see fig. 5-a. The purpose of this Worksheet is to help a person decide whether a job is Green, Yellow, or Red. The directions on the Worksheet should be self-explanatory.

When completing it, people should be specific, rather than general, when listing their responsibilities. So rather than a salesperson saying his or her job is selling (which it is, but for these purposes, much too general), in this exercise he or she should list specific things he or she is *doing* or would be doing. He or she might list things such as canvassing/soliciting for new business; making sales presentations; closing sales; preparing proposals; post-sale follow-up; customer service; paperwork.

JOB MATCH-UP WORKSHEET

Job Match-up is how well the key responsibilities of your job(s) fit your Greens, Yellows, and Reds. If you are considering a major shift in your responsibilities, do this Match-up exercise using those new responsibilities.

Write in your key (main/priority) responsibilities. Also, estimate the percent of time you are involved in it. When doing Match-up, ask yourself: *To what extent does that responsibility use my Greens?*

I. Key on-the-job responsibilities   % of time   MATCH-UP*
                                                                 (Circle one)

1. _____   _____   G   Y   R

2. _____   _____   G   Y   R

3. _____   _____   G   Y   R

4. _____   _____   G   Y   R

II. Key off-the job responsibilities
   Volunteer e.g. church, community, etc.

1. _____   _____   G   Y   R

2. _____   _____   G   Y   R

3. _____   _____   G   Y   R

                                          * G-a lot, Y-some, R-little

fig. 5-a

Taking information from the chart above, rate below (with a checkmark) the Overall Match-up of your Job I (on-the-job) and Job II (off-the-job), and your Greens, Yellows, and Reds.

Job I   Job II

_____   _____   GREEN: You will be using your Greens a lot, at least
                                  50% of the time. The job description is OK.

_____   _____   YELLOW: You will be using your Greens some, about
                                   20 % of the time. The job description needs
                                   to be changed to more Greens, fewer Reds.
                                   If not changed now, it should be changed
                                   within three to nine months.

_____   _____   RED: You will be using your Greens very little or
                                not at all. The job description should be com-
                                pletely changed or you should consider other
                                responsibilities that would use more of your
                                Greens.

fig. 5-a(2)

A household administrator might list (and it is never complete!): taking care of three children; preparing meals; shopping; attending events; transporting children; handling financial matters; maintaining/cleaning . . . to name a few things a homemaker might list. I just get out of breath listing them!

Jobs with similar titles often have different specific responsibilities, so it is important to find those out, rather than assume you know. So one way to evaluate a job (present or new) is to do the Job Match-up. Our calling includes USING our Greens and some Reds; doing the Match-up exercise is one way to determine how well a job does or does not do that.

JOB SATISFACTION INDICATOR

The JOB SATISFACTION INDICATOR is another way a person can evaluate his or her present situation or how well his or her job matches up with their Greens, see fig. 5-b. He or she can do this by asking himself or herself this question: Considering only your present job and what you do, on a scale of 1-low, 5-average, and 10-high, what is your present level of job satisfaction day-in, day-out?

So a person answers with a number ranging from 1 to 9; seldom does he or she say 10. Then I explain what the number means:

Answer: 7-10. This means the job is Green (uses Greens a lot); this person has a lot to be thankful for. Such people usually look forward to going to work and energized by what they do.

Answer: 4-6. This means the job is Yellow (uses some Greens). Usually life on the job is like a roller coaster, some days up—energized/excited; other days down—no energy, no excitement.

Answer: 1-3. This means the job is Red (uses Greens little or not at all). This is dangerous territory because the person is receiving way too little satisfaction, so their energy, excitement is low—no zip. Every day is a grind-it-out matter. Such people tend to be disgruntled and miserable people (I was in a Red job for three years) to be with, work with, and live with. See again By-Products of Red work, fig. 2-b.

JOB SATISFACTION INDICATOR

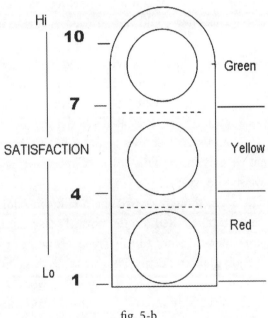

fig. 5-b

In Chapter 8, we will be raising issues significant to people who find themselves in Green, Yellow, or Red jobs. My goal with people is to help them be in work where their job satisfaction is 7 or above. The ramifications of Red work are too detrimental to people to be ignored . . . detrimental emotionally, spiritually, and perhaps (I emphasize perhaps) physically also.

Some people may be inclined to stay in Red work because it pays well, has good benefits, etc. But the question remains: Is a disgruntled co-worker a positive Christian witness? Is he or she glorifying God by remaining dissatisfied?

Having said this, for reasons unknown to us people, God may arrange circumstances to put someone in Red work to "clip his or her wings"—like an arrogant spirit, or sense of know-it-all, or feeling that there is nothing they would ever try that they could not succeed at (pride in its highest form).

Would God do THAT? I don't know. His thoughts and ways are beyond my thoughts and ways (as if you did not already know!). But what I do know is that His Word instructs us to be humble at all times and do our best as workers. So who knows, God may use a Red job to discipline us and in this process, awaken and jar us. As Hebrews 12:10 says: ". . . God disciplines us for our good, that we may share in his holiness." Food for thought . . . and if the shoe fits, we should wear it.

One more point, even though we will again talk about it in Chapter 8. A person may have to take a Red job temporarily (say up to 18 months maximum) to gain experience for a future Green job. Or he or she may take a high-paying Red job to pay off debts. But please, do this consciously and carefully . . . knowing in advance you are doing Red work. A tidbit: most people in a Red job start losing interest in it after six months on the job. They "cut it" the first few months because it is new, or they like the people, or they are getting good benefits, etc. But a Red job soon catches up with them around the six months point, or even before then.

If you have to (for good reasons) do this, please oh please understand fully that your level of job satisfaction will be low, and that is like trying to run a car on fumes.

Green work energizes . . . Red work "miserable-izes"

A Mini-Summary. I hope you now understand what Job Match-up means and how to evaluate a job with the Job Worksheet and/or Job Satisfaction Indicator. In this process, seeing the value of fitting the job to you and your Greens, rather than doing it the other way around—fitting you to the job. One of God's precious gifts to you is job satisfaction; it is up to us to do our best to be in jobs where our satisfaction level is at least 7. Green work is God-pleasing work and foundational to living out our calling.

2. IDENTIFY YOUR VALUES-PRIORITIES

As noted earlier, some people say Values, others say Priorities. Either way, they represent a person's or group of people's beliefs. To surface Values-Priorities, a person should ask at least two questions:

What is most important?
Who is most important?

In addition, develop reasons these "What is" and "Who is" are so important to you (or you and significant others).

And why are Values-Priorities important? They impact our decisions; they represent one way of making choices about what to accept or reject. Many years ago (in the dark ages) I turned down an attractive position because it conflicted with our family's Values. My friends thought I was crazy.

Values are individually developed; they are also family developed, which means a person may have to compromise at points in coming to a group Values decision. Values often determine a person's or family's lifestyle, including how they allocate their time, their talents, and financial resources as well as what it means to be Christ-like stewards of other things they own, e.g. residential property.

Values need to be pinpointed, clarified, and reviewed from time to time, otherwise the locomotive of life runs us over. Marvin, in his early thirties, said, "My father and I didn't have a relationship. He was always busy." Unlike Marvin, Bob, in his mid-forties, after his father died said, "I miss my dad. We were friends." My own father worked six days a week, but from my viewpoint that did not create any problems; I did not resent the long hours or feel neglected. I remember him as a warm, gentle, caring person. He encouraged me, trusted me, and seldom pushed me (Of course, I was such a "perfect" child!). While both my parents were busy, they had time for us kids.

Values, written or unwritten, represent our beliefs, which in turn directly impact our attitudes and actions. So we should take the time occasionally to consciously think through our Values and what the Word and Holy Spirit may be saying to us through them.

So in addition to the previous two questions, how should we go about surfacing our Values, and in what specific areas of our lives? In light of the fact much is already written about Values, let me make a suggestion or two (profound, of course!). I believe Values should be developed in at least two areas: one, Spiritual Values, and two, Other Life Values. Let's talk about Spiritual Values.

SPIRITUAL VALUES

I was preparing to give a brief account (in church) of my faith and what Jesus means in my life today. While doing this, I asked myself: "What do I really believe? What do I really believe about God?" Then it hit me. I value God; I value Jesus; I value the Holy Spirit; I value Scripture. Wipe away these values and my belief system disappears.

As I thought about including those words in my brief account talk, it almost sounded too simple. But the more I pondered those "value God, Jesus, Holy Spirit, and Scripture" words and what they meant, the more my heart warmed. I felt close to God, very close. So I included them.

Your Spiritual Values will be different, perhaps a whole lot different. What is significant is that they mean something to you, and as a result, help to keep you focused on Who is Most Important and What is Most Important.

So a way to surface your Spiritual Values is to think of Scripture that might trigger thoughts. For example, Matthew 6:33: "But seek first his kingdom and his righteousness . . . ." The words "first" or "his kingdom" and what they really mean might trigger Values-related thoughts. So a Value might be expressed as "To Seek God first" or "Live according to kingdom principles." You, I am sure, can think of other verses to represent your values.

One of my favorite Bible verses triggered the "I value God" idea. That verse is Hebrews 12:28: ". . . Let us be thankful, and so worship God acceptably with reverence and awe . . . ." I love that verse, especially the words reverence and awe.

OTHER LIFE VALUES

Here in LARGE PRINT (Not because you are a senior citizen!) are other Values areas to be considering; they are not meant to be in any prioritized order.

SUCCESS. Most people value success; sadly, few people have defined for themselves what they mean by success. Often people are carried along by what society or an organization calls success. We often call people successful who have done well in their organizations. Hmm. How does God view "done well"? How does that individual view success?

The dictionary defines success two ways. One, a favorable or desired outcome. Then it tails onto that definition these words (second definition): the attainment of wealth, favor, or eminence. Frankly, I want to be a "successful" Christian in terms of it having a "favorable outcome" (first definition) . . . now and in the future. I desire to be Christian. I value the Christian life.

But I just cannot relate to the second part of the definition; perhaps you can. There is nothing un-Christian about wealth, favor, or eminence . . . and aspiring for them. The question is: are your decisions about wealth, etc. God-glorifying? Are your motives God-pleasing? If yes, fine . . . and in the process of making it "big" financially and other ways, were you able to act Christianly at every turn.

Sadly, many people that I have associated with "at the top" often have regrets about how life has passed them by, in the process of getting to the top. They often ask: "Is this all there is to life? Now that I am here, what have I got"? It is regrettable hearing people say they have suppressed or kept covered up what they really wanted to do or admitting they never took the time to think through their Values and perception of success.

It is wrong to think about doing something significant at mid-life or at retirement. Our entire lives should be spent involved in significant-to-us work. Our call from God is for now, today, not 10 years from now.

I was in my early forties before I gave one speck of thought to how God views success. Before that, I was mainly concerned about moving up and then having a nice title and comfortable job . . . making good money, but not huge money.

Then I read a devotional reading by Oswald Chambers (page 210, My Utmost for His Highest, Dodd, Mead, & Company, copyright, 1935). There he compares God's view of success, and man's view. In a nutshell, man's view of success is reaching a goal. God's view of success is the process of reaching the goal, the process being to be *dependent* on Him now, *faithful* to Him now. He writes: "His (God's) end is the process—that I see Him walking on the waves, no shore in sight, no success, no goal, just the absolute certainty that it is all right because I see Him walking on the sea."

This reading turned my life around. I had to throw out many, many ideas and concepts that were good in man's eyes, but not in God's eyes. I virtually had to start over again. I threw out speeches I had written on success, goal setting, etc. My Life Purpose changed.

So I redefined and rewrote my definition of success: doing satisfying work, achieving my Life Purpose, being a responsible provider, being an available husband and parent, being a responsible Christian, and having a quiet time daily. Now that definition will not grab the headlines or see a horde of TV reporters banging on our front door. And while I may have "tweaked" it a bit over the years, the definition still holds.

So while you may view success as "moving up the ladder," remember, Jesus has no ladder, only a kneeling pad for us to use. He loves people equally at the top rung of the ladder, and at the bottom rung. He loves people with small and large investment portfolios. In any event, if in the *process* of doing any of these we consistently use a kneeling pad, then God will be pleased.

Besides clarifying and defining success, here are other Life Values possibilities, along with brief definitions. I would expect you to change and modify each one:

PERSONAL GROWTH-DEVELOPMENT . . . the feeling of
   improving as an individual.
FAMILY LIFE . . . the quality and quantity of time with my
   family.

LOCATION . . . the neighborhood and community where I live.

RELATIVES . . . their proximity.

CHURCH . . . opportunity to worship as I choose.

COMMUNITY and CIVIC GROUPS . . . opportunity to be involved.

RELATIONSHIPS . . . healthy, close (if appropriate), and as tension-free as possible.

ALONE TIME . . . to think, regroup, get refreshed.

The above listing is simply meant to get your Values wheels turning. Come up with your own listing. If you desire, label some A values, others B values. Put your Values and success definition in your Bible. Review them occasionally; change them as your circumstances change.

P.S. to this OTHER LIFE VALUES area. What I am going to include next really does not fit well in the Spiritual Values or Other Life Values areas, so I will include it here.

I think each person should think through what it means for him/her to be a *responsible decision maker*. So when appropriate, I ask these four questions:

Is it right?
Is it fair?
Will it help people?
Will God be glorified?

Supporting Scripture includes Proverbs 21:3: "To do what is right and just is more acceptable to the LORD than sacrifice." See also Proverbs 1:3. I use this four-question decision "grid" when product pricing, making a brochure, writing, and the like. In a nutshell, I value being a responsible, God-pleasing decision maker.

The main point I would like to make is: What does it mean for you to be a responsible decision maker at home, work, church, and the like? Perhaps developing some questions will help you, as it has me.

A Mini-Summary

Our Individual Calling includes realizing our Values, but Values we have seriously pondered. Life is so full of pressure that failure to surface one's Values usually causes lives and families to figuratively implode. Life is difficult, but "manageably difficult" with right Values and God's enabling resources. "His divine power has given us everything we need for life and godliness . . . ." 2 Peter 1:3.

3. CLARIFY YOUR LIFE PURPOSE-GOALS

What a dull subject: Life Purpose. Oh, at the surface it seems so much more exciting to talk about our passion and strategies to achieve stretching goals, etc. But wait a minute. Why are you here? Where are you heading? What are you aiming at? A specific, practical Life Purpose should address these questions.

Dull? Perhaps. Important? Yes, way up there in importance. And let us see what Scripture says. During a down time in my life, I felt something was missing. I couldn't put a finger on it. Even though I was functioning in my Greens, I was not up, fully excited, fully into what I was doing.

Then one morning in my office I read Ephesians 5:15 in Phillips translation: "Live life, then, with a due sense of responsibility, not as men who do not know the meaning and purpose of life, but as those who do." That is exactly the verse I needed. I had to admit I did not have a specific life purpose. Just knowing that made me feel ten times better. In the months that followed, I finally came up with something practical, which I will share with you in a moment.

It took me six months of going in circles, backing up, retracing steps, tossing into the recycle bin, etc. before I came up with the two essence questions about Life Purpose: **1. Who am I helping? 2. What am I Providing them**. See fig. 5-c.

So I wrote my Life Purpose: To identify the needs/problems of individuals and people in organizations, and solve them by (providing) profiling, advice, and training seminars. I also included doing this in business, non-profit, and Christian settings. So for me, the "Who was I helping?" answer would be people with needs and problems in areas of job and life direction.

LIFE PURPOSE WORKSHEET

The *goal* of this exercise is to develop a practical, down-to-earth statement that describes your "reasons for doing and/or being"—your reasons for doing what you do or want to do, or being the kind of person that you are or want to be.

While thinking through job options and specific job responsibilities, *use* the Life Purpose statement as a decision sounding board with this question:

To what extent will the responsibilities enable me to achieve my Life Purpose?

To *formulate* your Life Purpose, the essence questions to be asking yourself revolve around two issues: one, the people you desire **helping** and two, what you are **providing** them as you are helping them. The essence questions to be asking are:

HELPING: Who? How?

PROVIDING: What?

As you are thinking about these two questions, review your Interests and Concerns. And take a close look at your Positive Experiences Listing. In each case, try uncovering the kind of people you are helping and what specifically you are providing them.

So as you are doing this and thinking about "Helping: Who? How?," ask yourself: What kind of people am I helping? Be specific. For example, people lacking X-skills or Y-knowledge...or high-schoolers...or college students...or people about to retire...or sick people...or new employees in my organization...or home owners...or small business owners...or large company manufacturing people...or people I'm supervising, etc.

fig. 5-c

Then think through what you are "providing them." For example, you may be providing them technical assistance, or innovative designs, or encouragement, or information about_____, or construction assistance, or quality used cars, or specialty food products, etc.

Now write your Life Purpose in a sentence or two. Write it just like you would tell it to a friend. Be specific.

_____

_____

_____

_____

Example of Life Purpose: To help_____ by providing them technical information via on-site visits, monthly newsletters, and bi-monthly phone calls. Another example: To provide purchasing associates product and customer data via one-on-one visits, e-mail, and sending them appropriate industry practices.

Some people express their Life Purpose in two parts: one, their Do-purpose (Helping, Providing) and two, their Be-purpose...the kind of character qualities for which they are striving. One final word: a person usually modifies, refines, and re-expresses his/her Life Purpose as he/she continues learning, and attitudes and perspectives change.

fig. 5-c(2)

An informative place to begin is with your Positive Experiences Listing, which I also used as I developed my Life Purpose. See there who you are helping and what are you providing them. Fig. 5-c is designed to help you develop your Life Purpose.

So people you help may be students, or employees, or customers, or patients, or team X, and the like. It may be individuals, teams, or groups of people. Try to be as specific as you can. What you are providing them may be designs, a message you are propagating, research, hand-crafted reproductions, safe roads, etc. As I say to people when doing this: Let your mind (ideas-thoughts) hit the paper; and don't worry about "grammar" (grampa either) . . . it is not for publication, but for your use.

And I hope it goes without saying that since we spend a majority of our productive time on the job, our Life Purpose should be achievable there. If that is impossible or only partially achievable, then with careful planning, a person may achieve some of his or her Life Purpose goals in off-the-job settings, e.g. church, service organization, etc. I say careful planning because a person doing this may run into a time problem by spending too much time doing that (off the job), while not realizing some of their other personal Values.

As we have just seen, helping people is a key component of someone's Life Purpose. Let's see how people have the potential for helping people in different ways, depending on their Strategy, Tasks, Ideas, or Relationships tendencies.

HELPING PEOPLE . . . DIRECTLY OR INDIRECTLY

Generally speaking, everyone is supposed to help people, and most people want to help people. And it is also a Biblical concept. "Do not forget to do good and help one another, because these are the sacrifices that please God" Hebrews 13:16 (TEV). But because we have different areas of Satisfaction (Strategy, Tasks, Ideas, Relationships) and Skills, each person will tend to desire to help people differently. In other words, our Greens usually impact the way we help and help most effectively.

With this in mind, it is usually instructive to understand that people usually help others two ways: one, directly and two, indirectly. Let us for a moment zero in on this Directly/Indirectly Concept.

By "Directly" I mean a person is interacting a lot *directly* with people while helping them. Exhibit A of this would be many kinds of one-on-one responsibilities, e.g. counseling, visiting, socializing, mentoring, discipling, relationship building, encouraging, and the like. See fig. 5-d. In other words, most of their time on the job is spend *directly* with people, but only *indirectly* with other mediums like data, wood, designs, food, computers, paper, words (like I am doing now), and the like.

By "Indirectly" I mean interacting a little or some directly with people while helping them but usually a lot more not-directly-with-people stuff like words, numbers, products, machines, engines, instruments, computers, plastic, food ingredients, clothes, and the like. See fig. 5-e. What they do mostly is working with data or things, and so they help people *indirectly*. Let's illustrate this "Directly/Indirectly" Concept of helping people by describing how someone's Greens will impact how they help people. See again fig's 3-c, 3-d, 3-e, and 3-f, chapter 3. Let's start with Relationships people.

Generally, Relationships people tend to help people directly, whereas Strategy, Tasks, and Ideas people will tend to help people comparatively indirectly. So Relationships people will tend to be effective caring for patients in a hospital or home, or visiting lonely people, building relationships with key customers, or helping and encouraging youth. I repeat: Relationships people will tend to help people directly.

fig. 5-d

fig. 5-e

While not always the case, S, T, and I people tend to help people comparatively Indirectly. So an S person may help people by directing a manufacturing facility that makes a needed product through 700 people, and promoting it through advertising, meetings, etc. As administrative overseer, he or she spends lots of time analyzing financial operations, figuring out future strategies and goals, and the like. In other words, he or she spends less time directly with people, and more time directly with other stuff related to running a manufacturing facility.

Does S value people as much as R? Yes. Do they spend as much time with people as R? Usually not. But looking at things from the outside, who appears to help people more, R or S? Most people would say R because they do lots more one-on-one work with people. But S is helping people a lot, but Indirectly.

Let's go to Ideas people. They help people by inventing new products, or making new discoveries in a research laboratory. While doing this they usually spend most of their time at a computer, or researching new concepts, or sitting by themselves thinking and conceptualizing. Do they value people less than R? Absolutely not.

Here is the point I would like to make. The way we help people tends to be a function of our Greens. I spend very little time directly with people; I help people indirectly because I spend lots of time interacting with data and words, while perhaps only 10 to 15 percent of my time is working directly with people. Remember the source of our Satisfaction—in my case it is doing Tasks right, and in the process, doing lots of data analysis and problem solving. But I should not consider myself less of a people helper because you, a Relationships person, spend most of your time directly with people encouraging, counseling, etc.

Paul, a committed believer in his late 40s asked me: "Why don't I have a greater desire to do something for the poor or inner-city people?" Being "smart," I immediately looked at his Positive Experiences Listing. Not one of them had anything to do with helping the poor or inner-city people directly, or anyone else like that.

"Oh," he replied, somewhat relieved. "What should I do if I still want to help such people?" Good question, Paul. We both concluded after much discussion that if he were to give up his job and start working with such people full-time, he would be smack in his Reds. Secondly, we developed other ways he could help. They included: financially, helping them to start their own business (Paul was a Tasks person who owned a 35-person business, and making "good dough"), or doing some one-on-one work with them say up to four or five hours weekly as a volunteer.

Paul is "wired" by God to run a business, and run it efficiently. That is his Green. God's call includes using our God-given Greens. Today, Paul includes helping needy people as a Life Purpose, but doing that as a volunteer, not in his "job" job.

A Mini-Summary. Your Life Purpose should identify people you want to be helping. Depending on your Greens, you may do that Directly or Indirectly. All of us have to do both—work directly with people and directly with things. A Relationships person has to do the books and clean up messes occasionally. A Tasks person has to interact with people. With that in mind, none of us should feel guilty about not helping people when we spend the day doing statistical analysis, running a machine, or building a house.

I feel helped when our mechanic fixes our car. I myself was not helped, but the car was. I perhaps didn't even talk to the one who fixed it. But the "fixer" sure helped at the time of need, without talking to anyone. Who do car mechanics help? Car owners, and helping them Indirectly, rather than Directly.

One more point. Use your Life Purpose statement when considering a job change. Ask yourself: To what extent will those responsibilities enable me to achieve my Life Purpose. If your answer is "yes," then that job is a Green Light viewed through the eyes of your Life Purpose. If your answer is "no," then ask yourself: can I change my Life Purpose to include helping those kinds of people? But be careful as you do this. It is easy to lose our objectivity when something new arises that looks attractive. "Follow the ways of your heart . . . but know that for all these things God will bring you to judgment" Ecclesiastes 11:9.

CHAPTER SUMMARY

We began this chapter by saying life's pressures and expectations may see us "on the run" all the time, so the "temptation" to be leaning on other people's views of success, what they think important, etc., rather than thinking these things through for ourselves in light of Scripture and God's leading in our lives.

So we have stressed how important it is for us individually to do the Job Match-up, so that we will be more apt to be using our Greens and fewer Reds. Hopefully, you have thought through your view of Success and clarified your Values-Priorities, and lastly, surfaced the people you want to be helping and ways to help them consistent with your Greens and Reds.

Today I spent the morning at the hospital, having been called by a lady whose husband has cancer. She wanted me to visit him, pray with him, etc. They stopped going to church 30 years ago. God had been relegated to low priority, low Value in their lives. Guess who they are thinking about now? That is right, God. They have no support in terms of a church family.

This chapter about Job Match-up, Values, and Life Purpose may be dull reading. So be it. Sometimes what is really important may be dull, which should take nothing away from its inherent value. Hear again the words from Ephesians 5:15: "Live life, then, with a due sense of *responsibility* . . . as those who know the meaning and *purpose* of life." Life can be cruel. Jesus' executioners were cruel, but Jesus' goal was only to do His Father's Will and so please Him.

Life's realities are:

- Are you living responsibly?
- Where is your focus?
- Where is your hope?
- What is most important?
- Who is most important?

Our Values and Life Purpose, while doing Green work, will go a long way in giving us perspective when life's cruel side hits us . . . and it will, and unexpectedly. Just ask the widow of a recent cancer victim.

CHAPTER 6
STUMBLING BLOCKS TO LIVING OUT YOUR CALLING

The *goal* of this chapter is to point out **potential** hindrances and stumbling blocks to Living Out Your Calling.

REVIEW AND INTRODUCTION

The central thesis of this book is that it is a God-pleasing process to make decisions with God and you in mind. In other words, the first place we look is to God . . . to "seek Him first" (See Matthew 6:33) and during a decision process, rather than seek Him last or as a second thought.

The last few chapters have pointed to you . . . not in a selfish sense, but you in the sense of having a handle on your God-given Greens and God-given Reds. Also, they have pointed to you as one having the responsibility to think through your Values-Priorities and Life Purpose.

So while the focus of this book is on God and you, we know there are other factors that enter into a decision, such as what other people either expect or offer as wisdom or advice. So what I will be suggesting is that while we do not want to ignore what other people think, nor turn a deaf ear to them (not a relationship building exercise!), the fact remains it is usually primarily our responsibility to use our Greens and Reds wisely, as well as incorporate our Values-Priorities and Life Purpose into decisions. And we do this in a way not intended to turn off people, even though that may happen from time to time.

In this chapter, I will be sharing some potential hindrances or stumbling blocks to Living Out Your Calling. In other words, these stumbling blocks may, for example, prevent you from fully utilizing your Greens, or make it highly unlikely that you would achieve your Life Purpose.

As I share these, I do not want to come across as a "know-it-all" staring down people whose motives and intentions are to help, not hinder . . . encourage, not discourage. Instead, all I want to do now is to make you aware of areas that represent potential potholes, which if seen in advance, may help you avoid some unnecessary breakdowns along your life's journey. I have come to these conclusions after thirty years of helping people implement the Green Light Concept.

As you read through these potential hindrances, please keep an open mind. All of them may seem good at the surface; but I urge you to be careful. For example, you might welcome advice from someone you respect and trust as you think through your decisions and life direction. But the question remains: will the advice point you in a Green or Red direction?

Or if they give you advice without knowledge of your Greens and Reds, how much can you count on what they say? Even if their motives and intentions are "pure as gold," their encouragement may urge you to consider something really not consistent with your Life Purpose, or your Values, and the like.

I am very aware of Proverbs' instructions to enlist godly counsel and wisdom. What I am suggesting is that when considering issues related to your life direction, such people should know you first—your Greens and Reds, your Life Purpose, etc. It has been my experience that people giving advice usually do not know these things.

With these things in mind, I would like to share twelve things that may cause a person to make a wrong turn, or wrong decision, along life's up-and-down journey. View these as food for thought and information to include while trying to Live Out Your Calling.

1. LIVING OUT OTHER PEOPLE'S EXPECTATIONS

A person "lives out" other people's expectations when they do (within reason, of course) what someone else either suggests, expects, or personifies. Often their influence on our decision process is subtle, even unconscious, in addition to being conscious.

We may be unconsciously influenced hearing similar tidbits from several people about what we should be doing; then we read something that corroborates what these people said. Then—boom—we do it.

As I look back on how I decided to major in engineering in college, it really was an unconscious decision. My uncle, whom I respected, would tout engineers. A high school teacher said I was good in math, which she said was essential to engineering work. A neighbor "talked up" the good life of engineering, since her husband was an engineer.

In retrospect, I can see I was unconsciously influenced by these well-intentioned people. But my heart was not in math or engineering; I was really living out their expectations for me.

We may also be more consciously and directly influenced by one or two people. Listen to Ebony: "I am in teaching because my uncle feels that teaching is the most important job anyone can have. I respect him a lot, but I hate teaching." Together we discovered teaching to be one of her Reds . . . her Green was in a totally different field.

Lamentingly she adds: "I don't want to disappoint my uncle . . . he is so proud of me." She is still in teaching and still hates it. Parents, subtly and sometimes pretty directly, have things they expect of their children, especially what they should either do in life or major in at college. Often this puts a person (e.g. teenager) between a rock and a hard place, because people's advice and what a person knows about himself or herself is in conflict.

A doctor said to me: "In our family, you were expected to become a doctor, accountant, or lawyer; you had no choice. Besides, they were paying for our education."

Granted, there are times a person has no choice but to do what another says. But when there is a choice, we should be listening to our hearts, listening to God, and carefully heeding what our Positive Experiences Listing is telling us. Usually our Listing is screaming at us—"Do this (Greens), not that (Reds)." Will we heed its advice?

In a nutshell, maybe the right question to ask is "What does God expect of me?" The essence of what a person should be doing and expect of himself or herself is found in his or her Positive Experiences Listing.

So while we are all aware of the value of godly advice (Proverbs), I would urge you not to accept anyone's advice lock, stock, and barrel. But when such advice complements or adds to what you are already thinking, then thank God for such encouragement or confirmation.

2. MAKING VALUES-DRIVEN DECISIONS

Values-driven decisions means making life direction or job choices based solely or primarily on Values. In the last chapter, we dealt with the subject of Values-Priorities and their importance in decision making. You may recall we said Values are one important piece of information, not the *only* piece. An organized decision process includes Values, but also a person's Greens and Reds, and Life Purpose (sounds like our Individual Calling process!); in other words, at least three things, not just one thing, e.g. Values.

Often people do not want to face up to the notion that their chosen occupations are or has landed them in Red, dissatisfying work. So they think that by changing something externally to the job, it will fix the job problem.

So if a person values location—where he or she lives, then he or she assumes being there or living there will by itself make him or her happy. And that includes being much happier in their job. Bob valued the Colorado environment, including mountains. He disliked the Midwest, as well as his job there. So he and his family moved to Colorado and into a similar job, thinking being happy where he lives would make him happier on his job. But it did not.

Moving to Colorado was an OK thing to do; but a common mistake is to think that by realizing one's priorities and values—in this case location or where they live—they will also solve a job problem.

Similarly, this is true for other Values areas. Switching churches (assuming church is a value) will not solve a Red job problem. If a person in a Red job is having family relationship difficulties (often an outcome or by-product of Red work), then he or she may think buying a larger house will solve the problem. It will not. Nothing will change until the person changes jobs and goes into a Green job.

On the other hand, if someone is already in Green work, then making a Values-driven decision may work. So if Bob was already in Green work in the Midwest, and moved to Colorado and into a similar job, then his overall life happiness should be expected to improve.

In a nutshell, it makes sense to always use an organized, comprehensive approach to decision-making, not to make things complicated, but to arrive at a decision that takes many factors and variables into account. Life's complexities demand it; God's Word underscores it.

The next two stumbling blocks are closely related, but I hear each one so often and in different situations, that I decided to treat them separately for emphasis. I say this remembering our immediate goal is to help you or help you help someone else avoid making similar mistakes.

3. I-WANT-TO-HELP-PEOPLE MENTALITY

Like a Values Driven Decision, an "I-want-to help people" mentally means a person thinks THE MOST IMPORTANT thing in life is helping people . . . and helping people directly, not indirectly. So a social worker usually does a lot of direct people-helping. Right now, I hope I am helping people, but indirectly so. My means is words on paper, unlike a social worker working directly with people, using means like right questions, encouragement, counsel, and the like.

It is laudable to want to help people directly, few people would quarrel with its need and importance. But the question remains, will that kind of work utilize a person's Greens? So when a helping-people mentality puts one in Red work—well, by now you know the result—job and life unhappiness.

Ann is an Ideas person. She assessed her Green skills to include creating and designing room interiors. She can walk into a room, and in her mind, visualize room redesign options, in color no less (when I try to visualize anything, all I "see" is black space!).

Ann is a nurse. She said: "In my family, it was instilled in us that there was nothing more important to do than help people. So after much thought and deliberation, I went into nursing, thinking that epitomized helping people. But between you and me, I hate it."

Her Job Satisfaction Indicator was 3 . . . the Red zone. The reason for her dissatisfaction is that the job does not match her Green skills. Instead, she should help people indirectly while assisting a customer in designing room interiors, or something like that.

A word about Ideas people: Generally speaking, Ideas people are often naturally sensitive to people . . . they usually come across to others as empathetic and caring. So people naturally like them so they encourage them to go into "people work." But what people see, and what a person is on the inside, may be entirely different.

For some reason, lots of unhappy counselors come here for help, unhappy in their work. Many are Ideas people. And why are they unhappy? The job of mainly counseling and helping people is at best a Yellow for them, most likely a Red. Yes, they love people and want to help them, but they should help them while using their Greens.

I am generalizing now, but what I usually say to Ideas people in counseling is they could counsel up to 20% of the time; more than that and they usually get bored stiff. Why? The job of counseling is not mentally challenging enough for them. Besides, it usually does not use their primary Green Skills. A Tasks person may be able to counsel up to 30 or 35% of the time. A Strategy person should counsel people (as usually defined) perhaps 2% of the time, at most! A Relationships person usually has the most potential to counsel, assuming that counseling pops up in his or her Positive Experiences Listing.

Back to Ann, the nurse. Together we refocused her life. She literally had to start all over again. She had to change some of her Values, and very significantly, her Life Purpose. Now, several years later, she is bubbling over in Green work and happy she "bit the bullet" and made those hard choices and big changes in her life. God was on her side as she made difficult choices to change her career. Today, God is still on her side. God wants people to be satisfied. God wants people to use what He gave us—Greens and some of our Reds.

As we said in Chapter 4, we help people best when we are using our Greens in the helping-people process. Frankly, spending one-on-one time with people (my Red) is hard work for me; after I am done, I am pooped. I am pooped too after teaching a class (my Green), but it is a "pooped" full of energy. There is a big difference. Greens energize; Reds "miserable-ize."

4. I-WANT-TO-WORK-WITH-PEOPLE MENTALITY

People often say: "I want a job where I can work with people." Often this is a reflection of their Values, or being encouraged by someone saying they would be good "working with people." Or people say, "I am sick of job X (e.g. editing manuscripts or analyzing data and preparing reports). I want to work with people." And they mean it.

But there are people out there who have not thought through what they mean when they say "working with people." No one would question the nobleness or rightness of such desires. But here again, if a person does not ask the right questions, he or she may be headed in a Red direction.

And the right questions include: "What are you doing *specifically* as you are working with people?" or "What are the top two or three job priorities . . . the things you must do to do well in that job?"

You see, simply saying you want to work with people is too general. That is more a "values" statement rather than "job" statement (what you want to do). So when someone says he or she wants to work with people, he or she should also describe *specifically* what he or she wants to do.

For example, someone may go into sales work because he or she wants to work with people. But there are all kinds of sales jobs. Some sales work involves cold calling/cold canvassing. Others involve calling on the same customer many times over a six months period, and between times, spending lots of time coming up with a new product design and sales proposals. Some sales jobs are handled mainly on the telephone, rather than in person. Or a lot is done via e-mail.

A youth worker may go into youth ministry because he or she wants to work with people, but then the job really is one of organization and administration (Reds), rather than working one-on-one with youth building relationships, counseling, encouraging (Greens).

Here is the point. There are a thousand and one ways to work with people in any field or profession. Make sure you know what you will be doing specifically day-in, day-out in the process of working with people. Then match up the job with your Greens, as we did in Chapter 4. This way, you will avoid potential job failure, disappointment, and with it, lots of hassle.

Summarizing this sub-point: generally speaking, if we are responding to God's Universal Calling and Individual Calling, including using our Greens and achieving our Life Purpose, we should feel we are helping people. We should feel that way even if our head is buried in numbers and computers all day long, or our clothes get covered with grease from head to foot fixing mechanical equipment, or if we are painting on a canvas most of the time. God created you. Be thankful for what He gave you, both Greens and Red. Your biggest test in life may be maintaining a servant's heart as you paint, cook, fix, assemble, clean/wash, punch keys on a keyboard, and the like.

5. THE HARD WORK DOCTRINE

The hard work doctrine is a sacred cow. I am not attacking it or minimizing that hard work is essential to good performance in order to please God. But what gives me shivers is when people say: "Anyone can succeed at whatever he or she tries doing if he or she works hard, throwing himself or herself into it, and persevering." Professional motivational speakers love talking this talk. It sounds so true on the surface, but the concept has no depth, no substance.

Here we are not talking about marriage, relationships, and the like but work—job work. No one in his or her right mind questions the value of hard work. But saying that anyone can succeed at whatever he or she tries doing via hard work is not only wrong, but also life wrecking. Someone in Red work knocking his or her head against the wall every day will soon be a wreck.

Besides, no one can do anything or everything he or she tries. God created us with Greens and Reds, not all Greens. The Hard Work Doctrine is misleading. Hard work in Green work works. Hard work in Red work wrecks. Working hard in Red work temporarily is OK; working hard in Red work permanently is devastating . . . to our Christian walk, our witness, our relationships, to name just a few By-Products of Red work (See again By-Products, fig. 2-b).

Lots of people out there have worked themselves to the bone, only to end up frustrated and bewildered . . . or perhaps burnt out. Red work day-in, day-out will do a number on people. So do be careful. Work hard but it helps knowing in advance that what you are about to do is either Green work or Red work.

6. SIMPLISTIC FORMULA APPROACH

I do not mean to talk down to you now, but there are people who embrace very easy-to-understand formulas that ring hollow when it comes to their content and Finding Your Calling. Here is just one example:

Training + commitment + right attitude = success.

I personally value training, and understand the importance of both commitment and right attitude in order to do well. But to equate this with success may make for a good speech, but a lot more goes into success than training, commitment, and attitude.

When things like this are said or heard, I suggest placing such formulas alongside of our Individual Calling process. Applied to Green work, such a formula may serve as a good reminder or even encourager—a needed "shot in the arm" from time to time.

Rather than embrace the formula approach, I would suggest a person cull thoughts or phrases from Scripture and build his life around its teachings. "For everything that was written in the past was written to teach us, so that through endurance and the encouragement of the Scriptures we might have hope" (Romans 15:4). I wrote by this verse: "It is Scripture that is my primary encourager. So do your best."

A year ago, while doing Green work, I got discouraged and felt down. So I wrote myself a note (simple formula!). It said: "Do your best, you are serving God; He knows your heart." How much Romans 15:4 and my note to myself helped me get out of my funk, I do not know. But just thinking of Scripture and writing it down seemed to help; my attitude improved. But I think it was a lot more than that.

I believe the Holy Spirit functions in our lives in unpredictable, often unknowable ways. Referring to the Holy Spirit in the imagery of wind, John wrote (3:8): "The wind blows wherever it pleases. You hear its sound, but you cannot tell where it comes from or where it is going."

While simplistic formulas may help once in a while, we should be getting our main help from God's resources, remembering that the Holy Spirit comes and goes as He wishes, and does "immeasurably more than we ask or imagine . . ." (Ephesians 3:20).

7. THE EDUCATION-YIELDS-SUCCESS MENTALITY

No one would question the value of good education. But I see many people who, after graduation from college, often make decisions based mainly on their college major, rather than their Greens.

Here is what often happens. After graduation, a person enters the job market in the area he or she majored in at college, only to find out in the first two years he or she hates what he or she is doing in that field; it is Red—bright Red. But instead of changing careers and fields, he or she "hangs in," all the while really trying to get his or her money's worth from college or justify in his or mind he or she made the right choice in college. If he or she got good grades in college, a person seems even more reluctant to make the change into a more satisfying career and job.

Paul sold everything at age 35 and went to seminary, where his grade average was A minus. He finished among the top students who graduated. He had been pastoring a church for three years. He called because his Job Satisfaction Indicator was 2 (1-low, 5-average, 10-high). Yes, he was in a Red job. He said: "I thought since I got mostly A's in seminary, that the good grades confirmed my call to the pastorate. Now I realize this is not necessarily true."

So Paul and I developed a broader view of calling, that included what he felt was his call by God into the ministry. Now he is no longer in ministry as a church pastor, but is now in ministry for a parachurch organization AND in a Green job. Now several years later, he is still there, plugging away for Jesus . . . but in a ministry that fits his Greens.

Mark is a graduate mechanical engineer. As a Relationships person, his Greens suit him perfectly to be a supervisor for or executive director for a community service organization like United Way. His Life Purpose includes helping people who have practical needs, e.g. for food, or a home, and the like.

"I was the first in my family to graduate from college," he says. "I still think I can make it as an engineer. I worked hard to get my degree; I can continue working hard until I find my real niche in engineering." Mark, in his mid-forties, is everyone's friend; no one wants to hurt him. He had jumped from job to job. After we discovered his Greens and Reds, and developed his Life Purpose, he still could not fathom not being in engineering.

Because of his education, he views himself as an engineer, period. Yes, he is an educated engineer, but based on who God made him to be, he should be in a different field in order to be using his God-given Greens. Mark has yet to come to grips with whom he is; the roadblock is his education, in this case an engineering degree.

God values growth in godliness. "Train yourself to be godly" (1 Timothy 4:7b). I believe also that God values education that contributes to job and life success. But education is a means, not the end. Education that lines up with our Greens usually takes and has lasting benefits. People usually follow-up and use education that enhances Greens, broadening and further developing their Skills.

Education in our Reds tends to have limited value. So in the classroom I may learn the in's and out's of product promotion (my Red) . . . so gain a lot of knowledge about it. But like everyone else trying to do a Red, when I return home, I tend not to follow up or have much better promotion Skills after the educational experience. Promotion will still be a Red. As a principle, we should focus training in Greens, minimize training in Reds. We will discuss this a bit more in Chapter 11.

In a nutshell, we should be making decisions based on our Greens, and surround, support, and compliment them via Green-enhancing education. Then the Education-Yields-Success Mentality is most apt to come to fruition.

8. LOOKING WITHOUT KNOWING

"Looking without knowing" means a person starts looking for another job without first knowing what it is he or she wants to do. Sure, he or she may have some vague notions, but nothing specific. So he or she starts looking, hoping this might land him or her a good job. This is putting the cart before the horse.

Instead, a person should prepare first, then look. The Job Decision Checklist process, fig. 4-b, is one way to prepare. At the least, a person's preparation should include deciding the two or three options/jobs/positions that will best utilize his or her Greens and enable him or her to achieve his or her Life Purpose. Then when he or she starts looking for a job scanning ads, talking to people, etc., or hears about a job opening, he or she can compare that opportunity with the two or three options he or she has in mind at the start. This way, as he or she looks and listens, he or she can compare each job under consideration with his or her Greens, using the Job Match-up Worksheet, Chapter 5, fig. 5-a.

I find many people looking without knowing specifically what they are looking for. When asked why they are looking first, they usually reply: "I want to find out what is out there." People need to look, but be looking at each job opportunity in light of their Greens and Reds, not just whether it pays well or provides outstanding benefits.

9. SUCCESS PORTABILITY CONCEPT

The Success Portability Concept means success can be carried (portable) from one job to another. In other words, success in Job A virtually guarantees (within reason, of course) success in Job B because the person is successful now—in Job A. True sometimes. False oftentimes.

It works if the Skills required for Job A are similar to the Skills required to do well in Job B. But if the Skills required in Job B are different, watch out. A Red Job Match-up is in the making. Most of the time, the Skills required are different because the key/priority job responsibilities are different, often a lot different. And to make matters more difficult, often Job B pays more, sometimes a lot more. But we still must ask: Will Job B be a Green job or Red job? Will it enable you to realize your Values and Priorities? Will it enable you to achieve your Life Purpose?

Pastor Ted is associate teaching pastor at a church. His Greens include teaching, doing research, setting up and coordinating curricula and doing that especially for small groups. I am sure you can tell, Pastor Ted is an Ideas person and gets satisfaction from learning new concepts, grappling with theological issues, and seeing people grow spiritually. His present job is bright Green; he loves his work; he is achieving his stated Life Purpose, and realizing most of his Values, including Spiritual Values.

Then his denomination and minister "friends" started pressuring him to take on a new "challenge" and become a senior pastor of a 700-member church. Their reasoning, of course, was that since he is now successful, that he would be successful as a senior pastor.

Besides, they added, you need to "spread your wings," have your own church rather than work "under someone" (I hate that expression!). "You are ready to step up (I hate that expression too!)," they said. (Remember:

Jesus has no step ladder, so we should never view a job change as a step up or step down. Instead, view it simply as a change in responsibilities).

Together we went through the priority job responsibilities as that church's senior pastor. They included: speaking to large (often up to 800 people) audiences (teaching 30 people, which he is doing now and loves doing, and speaking to large audiences are very different skills); vision-casting and long-range planning; office administration; and supervising a large staff. We concluded the job of senior pastor required different skills . . . skills that were his Red, not Green.

This was one of the most pleasant consulting experiences of my life. Pastor Ted saw that being senior pastor was a Red job for him. His heart was in teaching and education, not public proclamation and administration. Pastor Ted declined the opportunity, grateful for the chance to take a look at it.

Pastor Ted's calling is to **Please God**, not to please people. While his friends thought they were helping Pastor Ted, if he had listened to them he would have been in a Red job. Let us stand and applaud Pastor Ted and his supportive/understanding wife right now (louder please).

You may say your life circumstances or the business you work for is different. If offered a job, you must take it or else. But the questions remain: "Who are you trying to please? What is your Individual Calling?" It is not about, "What will they say?" but "What does God think?" or "What would be a God-pleasing decision?"

Excellent salespersons often make average to poor managers. Average salespersons often make good managers. Why? The skills required in selling are usually a lot different than those required of a manager, and vice-versa.

All I am trying to point out here is you should avoid letting the attractiveness of a position, title, or money-making opportunity derail you from a Green job into a Red job. Success on Job A just might not be transferable (so portable) to Job B. Make changes with the Individual Calling process in mind, rather than being influenced too much by a job's title, compensation, and other factors.

10. MISUSING OR MISINTERPRETING PHILIPPIANS 4:13

Philippians 4:13 reads: "I can *do* everything [or all things] through him [Christ] who gives me strength" (emphasis added). The word often (not by you, of course) misused is "do." It is often misinterpreted to mean a skill like selling, speaking, administering, teaching, building, fixing, cooking, and the like.

Instead, the author Paul is saying that with Christ's strength, he could face (do everything) all kinds of tests, difficulties, trials, etc. The verse says nothing about skills. But what we could accurately imply is that while using his God-given Skills, he could, with Christ's help, make it, and so not be defeated or overcome by life's crushing blows. And Paul's life was filled with shipwrecks, storms, and other trials.

He said this kind of reliance on Christ's strength was the secret of his contentment in any and every situation (see Philippians 4:12). So Paul is not saying "I can *do* everything" because Christ would make him Super-person in terms of skills, talents, etc. What he was saying is that Christ would provide sufficient strength to face every life situation, good and bad. I like the way Today's English Version translates Philippians 4:13: "I have the strength to face all conditions by the power that Christ gives me." *Amen . . . thank you, Lord.*

In a nutshell, Philippians 4:13 does not wipe out the Green Light Concept by saying anyone can do anything. Instead, Philippians 4:13 gives us an encouraging promise of Christ's strength while we are using our Greens and Reds for His Glory.

11. MISUSING OR MISINTERPRETING COLOSSIANS 3:23

Colossians 3:23 reads: "Whatever you do, work at it with all your heart, as working for the Lord, not for men." In previous chapters we have pointed out the impossibility of doing something wholeheartedly day-in, day-out if a person's heart is not in what they are doing. Our hearts tend to be in Green work, not in Red work.

So a Relationships person's heart is usually not in paperwork, but in something directly people-related, e.g. building relationships, counseling, teaching small groups, etc.

A Strategy person's heart tends not to be in sitting at a computer designing new information systems. Instead, his or her heart might be in promoting a product or company to targeted groups of people.

Charlie, in his early 40's, sat in my office in tears. His Job Satisfaction Indicator was 3 (1-low, 5-average, 10-high), and it has been that way for several years. He said: "I have been trying to do my work 'heartily, as unto the Lord' for a long time. But it is like hitting my head against a brick wall. Nothing is changing. I am down all the time; it is tough."

Then he told me how everyone in his support group told him it was his fault he felt that way about his job, and that he should change his attitude and throw himself into his work "do it heartily as unto the Lord." But Charlie could not do that, because he was in Red work. He told me he felt he was being hammered down into the ground by Colossians 3:23.

No one intended to mislead Charlie. But they were misusing Colossians 3:23 because the cause of the problem was not Charlie's attitude, motivation, or commitment to Christ. The problem was he was in a Red job.

Charlie then discovered His Greens, using the tools described in Chapter Three. Armed with this information, he now has hope . . . not only of getting out of his Red job, but getting into Green work. Charlie is Finding His Calling and getting into work whereby he can genuinely carry out what Colossians 3:23 instructs us to be doing.

12. DICTATING HOUSE PAYMENTS

This hindrance to Finding Your Calling and living out a God-pleasing life could refer to any kind of unusually large financial obligations, which raises its ugly head in those things we call monthly payments. Examples are numerous: car payments, vacation spending, house payments, etc. But because large house payments are often a common problem, I am going to use that as our example of large financial obligations.

When my wife and I bought our first home in Kansas City in 1961, our house payments were $150 a month, and I was making a grand total of $450 a month (before taxes). Our house payments were *dictating* our life, our decisions, etc. It was driving me crazy.

We overbought, paying $21,500 for the house. Three years later we moved to New England. Our first decision was to pay no more than $16,500 for our next house (We actually paid $16,800. Close enough!). But then we "started to live," away from the pressure and stress of large, uncontrollable monthly financial obligations. Boy, did we learn the hard way! And, we lost money when we sold our Kansas City house.

Today, I see a lot of young people/families doing as we did in Kansas City—overbuying, usually in anticipation of making a lot more money in the near future. They come here for consultation stressed out or as they say, "burned out." They are financially strapped down between a rock (huge house payments, not to mention two car payments) and a hard place (Red job). They purchased their house (often dream house), in anticipation of a better job, and in that process, paid no attention to their God-given Greens, etc.

Dream houses seldom lead to dream lives. Expenses always (yes always) go up, never (yes never) down. Instead, dream houses often lead to an almost wild, out-of-control life and lifestyle. Does this please God? You answer that for yourself.

Nine times out of ten, the husband is in a Red job. If two incomes are necessary to support a lifestyle, and the wife is also in a Red job, it is doubly difficult. When we pinpoint someone's Greens to determine what he or she should be doing, it often means change . . . change of job, occasionally companies, and his or her chosen occupational field, as well as a change to a more simple life, simpler tastes, and the like. The field we identify as his or her Green field is most often not a high-paying field (Isn't that always the way?).

To avoid this depressing scenario, we should initially be thinking through our Calling, and what is important in God's sight, then adjusting our lives to be consistent with our Greens, which may also mean adjusting our lifestyle, including size of house and other purchases, to the realistic income potential of that Green job and field.

We did that after getting to New England early in our marriage; we never regretted those decisions. And we still live (now over 40 years) in our $16,800 house. We put an addition on it many years ago so when I stretched my legs in our living room, my feet would not hit the person sitting opposite me.

Large, unnecessary financial obligations may hinder a person from Finding their Calling. Everyone? No. Many people? Yes. For most believers, life should not consist of size of house or number of cars in the driveway.

Instead, life is being the kind of Christian you in your heart know you should be and want to be NOW, right now. And that includes the kind of witness you are when you are sixth in line at the grocery checkout line, or while visiting your doctor, or asking your mechanic about the condition of your car.

Change is difficult, often painful (including tough on the pocketbook . . . expect to lose money). But ask yourself: What will please God? What are my Spiritual Values and to what extent am I realizing them now? When making any kind of change in lifestyle, job, etc., I urge people to consider forming a three-person prayer team they can go to with their specific requests. For example, requesting their prayers at the time of a job interview, or during a decision time, or while clarifying Values and Priorities, etc.

I believe were it not for five ladies who prayed for me each week and oftener, I would not still be in business today. And you know what? I hated telling them my prayer needs; they sounded like things I should know or should be able to do myself, without their help. How wrong I was. Some of us think we do not need others, and perhaps more so, that we really do not need God. When, oh when will we ever learn!

CHAPTER SUMMARY

People give advice because they care, make purchases to benefit their families, make decisions because they really want to be "responsible citizens." For the most part, they are doing nothing unethical, immoral, or sinful. People generally want to do what is good and what is right.

You have heard the saying: The good is the enemy of the best. The good is what is good in man's eyes; but God expects the best, our best, and that includes our best effort to fully realize our Calling, and be the kind of believer He wants and we know down deep in our hearts we should be. Unknowingly, a person may settle for what is good, to the encouragement and applause of most people. However, the good may hinder someone from Finding his or her Calling.

The battle rages every day. Our human nature fights the Spirit of God tugging lovingly and mercifully on our hearts and wills. Our human nature desires what is good; God desires for us what is best. "No man can serve two masters." (Matthew 6:24.) The best means entire surrender of the things we see, and total commitment to what we do not see. And therein lies the daily battle.

> Colossians 3:1-2 ". . . Set your hearts on things above . . .
> Set your minds on things above, not on earthly things."
> 2 Corinthians 4:18 "So we fix our eyes not on
> what is seen, but what is unseen."

Think of it. God knows everything; you know only a speck. God knows you; you know a drop about yourself. God desires the best for you. He wants you to be completely devoted to Him. Be aware of hindrances that represent potential potholes to Finding Your Calling. God can be trusted; He is trustworthy. Are you trusting Him? Is it your heart's desire to please Him? Give Him your answer, and then do not tell a soul. Your relationship with Him is precious . . . let Him be your Confidant.

CHAPTER 7
A TRANSITION: DEALING WITH REDS

The *goal* of the chapter is to give you some tips on how to DO something that uses your Reds . . . and do it the best you can and with the right attitude.

INTRODUCTION

This chapter is a transition from Section one: "Understanding your calling and what God desires" to Section two: "Living out your calling and what God desires." We are going from Idea and Concept (Section One) to Application (Section Two)—applying or acting on what we are learning. When we put into action these principles, we most likely will be using our Greens and Reds.

Since many people often have difficulty just getting started doing something Red, or when they do start, only do a half way job (and sometimes do it with a poor attitude), we need to deal specifically with Reds if we are to in fact do Reds (take action) and do what is required as well as (not halfway) possible.

All along, we have been saying our Individual Calling includes using our Greens <u>and</u> some of our Reds. Just to refresh your memory, someone doing Green work usually initiates action on his or her own . . . he or she is on "go." On the other hand, someone doing Red work usually "slows down," even "stops" (or never gets started in the first place).

So Reds may create problems for us. Not only do we usually not do them very well, but we tend to put off doing them until later, tomorrow, or next week. Or we rush through them like a madman, often later regretting the quality (lack thereof) of the work or the way we treated people (unkindly, or talking rudely to someone) while doing something we dislike doing.

Recall from Chapter 2 the "No Perfect Job" concept, and that up to 40 % of what we do might be spent in Red work (40/20/40 Concept, Chapter 2). For example, Emily, a writer (her Green is Ideas) spends 30% of her time doing creative writing, a Green for Emily. She also spends 25% of her time editing (making corrections and changes in grammar, sentence structure, etc.). Editing is her Red.

Reds exist. Everyone has Reds. Rather than deal with Reds as Reds, many people go into contortions and do gymnastics (figuratively) trying to turn a Red into a Green. In all my years in this business, I have not seen it happen yet. People may say they did, but I seriously doubt it. Feedback from hundreds of people, plus my own experience indicates the best way to handle Reds is to simply deal with them as Reds and go from there.

We all wish we did not have them. Someone driving a car in a rainstorm wishes it would not rain so hard. Wishing will not cause raindrops to stop falling so hard. Neither will wishing we did not have Reds turn them into Greens, as if we had "magic wand" power over them.

There are things in running this business I dislike doing because they are Reds. And even though once in a while I may hate them less, over the years it seems Reds do not get easier to do, in fact, many tend to get harder to do. I still hate doing (because they are my Reds) paperwork, billing customers, answering correspondence, and handling finances.

So Reds are, whether we like it or not. So like driving a car in a rainstorm, we must deal with them, rather than try wishing them away. The goal of this chapter is to give you helps in Dealing with Reds in a practical, realistic manner so that your overall performance will be a "solid" B, if not close to or at A levels.

A QUICK REVIEW

It is always well to remember the following about GREENS and REDS:

A person tends to do GREENS well (A or B+ levels) and receive satisfaction while doing Green work. Doing Greens is like fueling an engine; a person is energized by the "fuel" sense of accomplishment. They "go."

A person tends to do REDS not as well (C or D+ levels) and receives little or no satisfaction while doing Red work. So there is no "fuel" to energize a person. In anticipation of doing a Red, a person often "stops"—hesitates, puts it off, or starts doing anything but that Red job.

A reminder: as usual, we are considering only time-consuming, ongoing tasks, not five-minute or infrequently done tasks.

At the outset, let me quickly say five things . . . keep these in mind as you read this chapter.

1. Many, many Reds are doable, if we will deal with them realistically, rather than with a wish-I-didn't-have-to attitude, such as we exhibit when eating brussel sprouts or liver.
2. We usually do not do Reds well. We will offer suggestions to help you do many Reds at B or better levels, rather than at C or D+ levels.
3. Do not try to gloss over your dislike for a Red by saying to yourself or trying to convince yourself you really should not or cannot dislike a Red. Instead, accept your Reds; my Reds may be different from yours, but I too have Reds to accept.
4. Reds are a primary reason people procrastinate. I put off cleaning our basement for 10 years. I finally did it when I knew we were having house guests for two weeks (we put unruly guests in the basement). Then, of course, I could not find anything!
5. Reds may cause people to "erupt like volcanoes;" our fuse gets short doing Reds for too long at a crack. See again "By-Products of Red work," fig. 2-b. Since our goal is to do things that glorify God, we have to take measures to prevent these eruptions or reduce their frequency and intensity.

IDENTIFYING SOME OF YOUR REDS

You probably already know your Reds. But if you do not know them or are unsure, here is a way to pinpoint some of them. Simply list some of your life's Negative Experiences.

A NEGATIVE EXPERIENCE is any past experience that was dissatisfying because you:

> Had **little** or **no interest** in it
> Had **little** or **no desire** to do it
> Did **not** do it **very well,** in your opinion

Negative Experiences give off **few feelings** of **accomplishment** and **satisfaction**. As you can see, a Negative Experience is just the other side of a Positive Experience, which we used to pinpoint your Greens. No wonder we procrastinate when faced with something we have little or no interest in, or desire to do, then on top off it all, usually do not do very well. And the reward for doing it is little satisfaction (except being glad it is over with until next time you have to do it!).

Some of my life's Negative Experiences include: gardening; thermodynamics course in college; being a design engineer; selling; plumbing and electrical projects; promoting anything to a group of people; mechanical work of any kind, especially cars; a lot of socializing at one time; doing our taxes; to name some of them.

As mentioned above, accept your Reds. To say something is Red says nothing about how important it is to do, or that this gives you an excuse not to do it. I say, "Nothing of the kind." So if entertaining people in your home is a Red, accept that. Or if greeting people as a church greeter is your Red, accept that. If cooking or baking is your Red, accept that. Or if speaking to large audiences is your Red, accept that. It will go a long way to enabling you to deal with it realistically, and I hope in a God-pleasing manner.

A KEY ENABLER: THE "SPILL OVER" CONCEPT

So if we have little interest in and desire to do Reds, how do we get them done, rather than procrastinate? How do we do them well, preferably at B+ or A levels, rather than just do it at C levels? Do we just say "God help me" and expect Him to supply all the power to do it? Far be it from me to say to you, "No, that is not the answer." You may have done this on an occasion or two, and found it helpful. But remember, here we are talking doing something time-consuming, and ongoing, not something for brief stints or once a month.

But for me, and lots of other people, the answer lies in our being responsible "Dealers with Reds" and "partnering with" God—asking for His help and grace, in the process of doing them. Believe me, we need Him, but we also need to do our part, which is to do our very best.

And a key enabler to doing our part in a responsible manner lies within The Spill Over Concept. See fig. 7-a. Use your imagination as I describe it. As you know, when a person is doing Green work, they generate satisfaction/energy—in so doing, fill up their "fuel tank." When I do in-company consulting, because it is Green-for-me work, I "fill up." I return to my office up/energized/excited.

When I dig into Red work waiting for me at my office, the energy/fuel from doing Green work "spills over" into my Red work. I am usually more apt to tackle it in the right frame of mind and do it fairly well, for a time at least. In fact, I get it done, rather than let it sit there.

Said differently, I can draw on my Green fuel to energize me while doing Reds. But like a car's fuel tank, it soon runs out. Again, like a car, I need to refuel (gas up) by doing Green work. Without enough Green work (refueling excursions), trying to do Reds is like "running a car on fumes"—we lack energy, zip, etc.

This Spill Over Concept means responsible people have the capacity to do Reds, and as we shall see shortly, do them fairly well, and in this process of applying the Spill Over Concept, asking God for His divine help and enablement.

Said simplistically, Greens replenish, Reds deplete. Greens generate, Reds "burn it up." This process should be ongoing: replenishing, depleting, generating, burning. The fuel satisfaction is replenished doing Green work. It is depleted doing Red work. Our Individual Calling includes DOING Green work and Red work. Keeping in mind and implementing The Spill Over Concept is one way to do this.

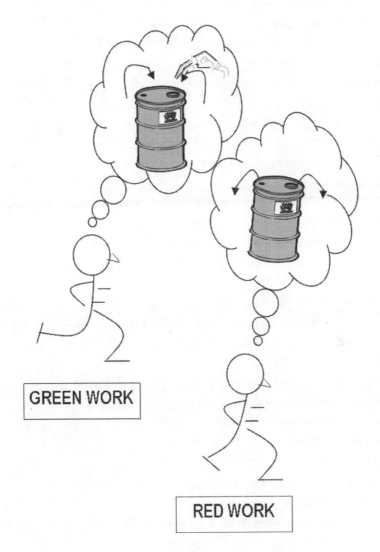

GREEN WORK

RED WORK

fig. 7-a

WHY DID GOD GIVE US REDS?

Let's pause for a moment and ask: "Why did God give us Reds?" Looked at differently, we may sometimes wish He had given us all Greens. Why did He create us this way, with Greens and Reds? I don't know and never will know. However, let me advance **four hunches.**

One, Reds help us *appreciate our Greens more.* Here is what usually happens. There is Red work to do, quite a bit in fact. So I dive into it. Then the Green fuel tank empties, and the Red work turns doubly difficult . . . a grind. But I finish it. Then when I "hop back" and do Greens, I usually do so with a totally different attitude and outlook. I look forward to work, Green work, rather than dreading work, as I do when doing Red work. Without Reds, I would most likely take my Greens for granted, and not really appreciate them as I should.

Two, Reds help us *appreciate other people more.* When I am doing my Greens, there are other people to "fill in the gaps" (my Reds). I am surely glad other people know how to do well what is for me Red work, like fixing cars, selling a product, promoting a program, managing finances and investments, fixing computers, and the like.

Not only do I appreciate other people's Green Skills, but it contributes to my appreciating them more as people. I do not have to envy what they can do well or go around wishing I was as "gifted as they." I accept that their Greens are my Reds.

This "appreciate other people more" concept also spills over into what teamwork is all about. That is, each person carries his or her Green load towards a common goal. And in the process, he or she usually does different jobs.

Three, Reds contribute to helping to *keep our pride in check.* Just think, if a person could do just about anything, he or she just might walk around with his or her nose in the air (and stumble a lot tripping over raised sidewalks and fallen tree branches!). It takes a humble soul to admit, from the heart, that something that "looks easy" is a Red.

For example, socializing and making small talk looks simple and is simple, for some people, and not for others. I have been sincerely laughed at telling some people that socializing is my Red. They look at me with this "you must be kidding" look and smile. Oh well.

You see, I encounter lots of people struggling . . . almost in desperation, erroneously applying Philippians 4:13 and its "I can do anything through Christ" concept. Recall we discussed in the last chapter: Stumbling Block 10, how many people misapply Philippians 4:13. Our ego and pride prods us to look superhuman, or at least somewhat better than our peers. We are not superhuman.

Instead, we are creations of God . . . fit together by Him according to His Ways, not our ways. And are not His Ways higher than mine are? (See Isaiah 55:9.) And His Way includes Greens and Reds.

Four, Reds remind us of our *humanity, our limited capacity*. In turn, this should turn our attention to God, realizing again and again and again how much we need Him. Yes, we need God's help at every turn, whether doing Green work or Red work, when our goal is to live all of life in a God-pleasing manner.

Most people would agree, however, that we need a special measure of God's Spirit, empowerment, and enablement when we tackle something using our Reds, with or without the Spill Over Concept. The fact is we are different people doing our Reds; I don't like that person (myself) when doing Reds.

Red work has the potential to bring out the worst in a person—their worst attitude, reactions, etc. Therefore, we need a double measure of His special grace. Ephesians 6:18 says: "Pray . . . on all occasions." I add—pray for help while doing Green work but also especially so doing Red work.

Summarizing: I hope these four hunches at least crack open the lid on answering the question about why God gave us Reds. I hope we agree that God kept you in mind when He made you; it is up to us to keep God in mind by letting Him be God, treating Him as God, and taking ourselves off the pedestal of thinking we are god and can do anything at any time.

SETTING THE RED STAGE: WHEN WE HAVE A CHOICE

Let's set the stage for responsible Red action by saying sometimes we have a choice whether or not to do Red work, at other times we do not. For situations when a person has a choice, I have developed Four Questions to ask oneself to help someone decide whether or not to do a Red-for-him or her task before automatically saying "yes" (which responsible people often tend to do) or "no" to the opportunity. I realize at the outset a lot more than this goes into any decision, but let us narrow our focus on this one issue: Should I do that Red-for-me task I am being asked to do? Here are the four questions:

1. Is the task <u>SIMPLE</u> or <u>COMPLEX</u>?

Generally speaking, the simpler the task, the more doable is a Red. The more complex the task, the less doable is a Red. Then to top it all off, a Red task (including simple ones) usually turns complex after doing it several days straight.

Wallpapering a room is a simple task, and for most people, more doable than a complex task like deriving mathematical formulas or developing computerized models of diesel engines. But watch out! If wallpapering a room is a Red, what appears to be a simple task may turn complicated after four straight days of it. A simple task like typing letters (if someone's Red) may turn complicated after two straight days of it.

And Reds often do a number on relationships. Ever talk to a married couple discussing what happened as they teamed up to wallpaper a bedroom? It is called arguing . . . Red rage!!

Remember: what is simple to one person may be complex to another person. To me, reading a recipe is not simple, plus I don't know the lingo very well. To someone in his or her Greens, it is simple (within reason, of course). I read "simple" instructions about how to repair or put together something mechanical. To me, those "simple" instructions are complex. I have to read them 10 times before it even begins sinking in; sometimes there is no sinking in at all!!!

So, before making a decision, one question to ask yourself is—Is the task simple or complex? A simple-to-the-person task tends to be more doable . . . for a time, at least.

2. How <u>PUBLIC</u> is it?

A public task is done for or before hundreds of people. Exhibit A of this is public speaking to say, 300 or more people, or writing a 30-page or longer publication to be read by thousands of people.

The other side is a private task, usually done in a small group setting or better yet, one-on-one with someone. Exhibit A of these would be tutoring someone, or visiting a lonely person. Red public tasks tend to be less doable than Red private tasks.

Public speaking is a Red for Paul. He did no public speaking in his Positive Experiences. What happens when people like Paul say "yes" to giving a 20-minute speech to a 300-person audience?

It goes something like this. Five or so days beforehand, he starts getting more and more nervous, edgy, feeling increased pressure and stress (negative stress . . . see By- Products, Chapter 2, fig. 2-b). Say the wrong thing to him a day or two before the scheduled speech and it "sets him off." Bang, hand me the earplugs, please!

Then after the speech he tends to be wiped out, bushed, worth nothing for two days at least. People doing something in their Reds are not bad people; simply good-intentioned people trying to do their best and do their part. Now tell me, is what happened God-pleasing? Were they able to conduct themselves Christianly? Could a relationship have been torn in two during their five-day countdown to giving the speech?

It is my belief God was neither pleased nor honored by those seven plus days revolving around giving a 20-minute speech. So is it desirable for the Paul's of this world to automatically say yes to doing such things? My answer: perhaps once in a while, but not monthly or quarterly. I do not believe their calling would include doing public Reds like speaking to large groups a lot.

It is often said that people rise to the occasion. I would like to submit that people are more apt to "rise to the occasion" in a God-pleasing manner for a Green occasion rather than for a Red occasion. H-m-m. Think about it, at least.

Assume visiting lonely people is also Paul's Red. It would seem best for the Paul's of this world to do something private, rather than something public by responsibly preparing for and doing something like visitation, rather than public speaking to large audiences. While still not easy to do, something private would be less difficult to do than something public.

We will cover questions 3 and 4 quickly because to go into any depth would be a lengthy exercise.

3. *Will other people's* WELL-BEING *be* ADVERSELY AFFECTED?

A person may be well-motivated and sincere, but the effects or results of his or her efforts while doing Red work may adversely affect other people (those being influenced or helped) in such areas as health, safety, personal development/growth, and the like.

So I should not volunteer to fix (my Red) the car brakes for a needy person; they would crash at the first stop sign or sharp corner. When a willing volunteer teaching a class of 40 people does a poor job of teaching, it may either impede or frustrate eager learners for a long time. In such a situation, the teacher may be better off teaching a small group of three to five people, perhaps.

4. *Could it (doing a Red) negatively impact the organization's or person's* CREDIBILITY?

For example, if being chairperson of an interdisciplinary task team is someone's Red, he or she will tend not to do it well. In turn, his or her credibility in the eyes of his or her peers may go down. Similarly, if someone (doing Red-for-them work) representing an organization performs poorly, it often has negative effects on the organization's credibility. It may take years to build personal and organizational credibility, but only 10 minutes to tear it down.

Summarizing these four questions . . . God's Individual Calling includes using our Greens and some of our Reds. Why some of them and not all of them? Some Reds, because of the four issues we just raised. As we have seem, Reds have the potential for causing negative ripples or causing us to be less-than-Christian in the process of doing them.

FOUR PRINCIPLES FOR DOING REDS

Let's turn to the situation where you have no choice but to do what will be for you Red work. You may have chosen to do the Red work (after going through those last four questions, of course!), or you simply have to do it because someone else in authority said to, or because of your circumstances, you have no choice but to do it.

So, given the fact you have Red work to do, here are four principles to help you bring Red work into realistic focus. Some of these we have already touched on before, but here is a place to bring it all together. Now, to the first principle:

1. Form <u>REALISTIC</u> <u>EXPECTATIONS</u> about Red work. So expect:

a. Little satisfaction from it, except to be glad it is over with until next time.

b. To lack confidence, both during preparation and implementation.

c. The task to turn complex. A "user friendly" computer software program may turn "user hostile" after five straight days of it.

d. To battle procrastination.

e. To make mistakes.

f. To have difficulty keeping focused.

2. <u>BALANCE</u> Green work and Red work.

This is our friend the 40/20/40 Concept. Every job has Greens and Reds. So try having enough Green work . . . at least 40%, while responsibly doing Red work. Again, Greens refuel, Reds drain.

3. Relate Reds to your <u>LIFE PURPOSE</u>.

A person should think of how doing Reds might contribute to realization of his or her Life Purpose. Writing is my Red. However, I am relating this Red work to realization of my Life Purpose. It does not make doing Reds any easier, but it helps me keep going!

4. Keep other people's <u>ENCOURAGEMENT</u> in perspective.

After taking on a Red task, someone may say with the purest of motives to encourage you: "I know you will do a great job." This communicates one thing to a person: A-level performance and meeting the deadline. Once a person internalizes what he or she is being told, he or she may feel pressure and perhaps stress.

Do not let other people's encouragement, well-intentioned as it is, upend setting realistic expectations (Principle One, above). Graciously (with a smile too, of course!) accept their encouragement, then do your best, with God's strengthening enablement. It is time for action.

SIX GUIDELINES FOR DOING REDS

The following six Guidelines should help a person DO a Red fairly well, assuming it is reasonably doable (and not overly complex) Red—hopefully at a B+ level, if not A level. Without these Guidelines, a person can expect to do C or D+ work (of course there are exceptions) over the long haul. Again the reminder: we are considering mainly time-consuming, ongoing responsibilities, not five-minute tasks done once a week or twice a month.

1. PLAN PLUS.

This is the **big** one, the **important** one, if we are to do Reds at B+ or A levels. Plan Plus means allowing and scheduling more time than first anticipated to do the Red, because Reds usually take longer to do than we first thought.

So it may take two or three times longer for someone to do task P when it is his or her Red, compared to someone doing it using his or her Greens. Why? The culprits we have just been describing: the task will turn complex, battling procrastination, making mistakes, having difficulty staying focused . . . to name some of them. So a person should expect a Red task to take longer, much longer than first anticipated.

To illustrate: if it takes a Green worker one day to wallpaper a room, it will take a Red worker at least two days to do it as well as Green. Red could do it in one day, but the results will show it!

If painting house windows is your Green and my Red, you can paint a window in one hour "perfectly." It would take me at least three hours to do it as well (or at least almost as well). A salesperson functioning in his Reds will have to call on twice as many people as someone in his Greens to make enough sales. So he must plan for that—Plan Plus.

Here is a rule of thumb. Green job, Green time. Red job, Red time—double or triple the usual/Green time. There is no way to rush important, time-consuming Red tasks and complete them to Green standards. So we must allow more time for them. In other words, PLAN PLUS—allow and schedule enough time to do it and do it well.

Just think. Most people, myself included, usually underestimate how long it will take to do something. If I ask you how long it takes to get from where you are now to downtown, you might whip out 30 minutes. In all probability, it will take at least 40 minutes. I will estimate it will take 45 minutes to do paperwork (my Red). I finish two hours later. So think for a minute how far behind and frustrated a person can get by not scheduling EXTRA TIME to do Red work.

So responsible people will usually do Reds best by planning at the outset it will take more time to do than first anticipated—Plan Plus.

2.START ON SCHEDULE; TRY COMPLETING IT

START on schedule (or do it now); try <u>COMPLETING</u> it (or get to the appropriate sub-goal). We human beings often look for excuses before starting Red work, such as "It is too hot" or "It is too cold," or "I am not ready," or "I might bother them," and on and on. So, if doing administrative work is a Red, or writing a letter to missionaries is a Red, a person might start thinking of people he or she should call, or a person to go see, rather than do the Red work NOW.

Or someone may secretly wish for an interruption . . . a visit or telephone call from someone, in hopes of delaying starting, then "blame him or her" for not getting it done in a timely fashion. We are all prey to these seemingly innocent excuses and interruptions.

Then after starting and half-way through something, our minds start wandering, thinking of other things we *should* be doing, forgot to do, etc. Resist the temptation to stop half-way through . . . try completing it. It is better to complete it 75% of the time, rather than 10 % of the time. Letting things "hang" half-done is a bad rut to get into. Someone said: "Doing a Red is like taking bad-tasting medicine. Do it right away, and get it done; delaying only makes matters worse."

These first two Guidelines are the important ones. The next four are "quickies," some of which we have already hit on.

3. USE THE BEST TOOLS/EQUIPMENT AVAILABLE.

Poor equipment will only frustrate a person more, increasing the error probability, and giving him or her another reason to procrastinate or only give half-effort to doing something well.

4. PACE BY SWITCHING.

This means alternating Green and Red tasks, at least when it is reasonably possible to do so. This way we will be applying the Spill Over Concept. So if counseling individuals is a Green, and paperwork a Red, a person is more apt to do his or her paperwork right after getting fueled up from counseling.

5. HOLD YOURSELF ACCOUNTABLE.

This means a person holds himself or herself responsible and accountable, rather than expecting others to be constantly prompting and encouraging him or her. And here we are talking of doing Red tasks, not about others holding someone accountable in other areas of his life.

In this process, exercising self-discipline to start on schedule, then staying focused on the task at hand, as well as keeping in mind how the Red task may contribute to his or her Life Purpose, and the like.

6. ADAPT YOUR METHODS OR APPROACHES TO USE YOUR GREENS, SOME AT LEAST.

A task may have only one way to complete it. Or an organization requires a certain way. If so, then this Guideline can not be applied. However, there may be tasks and situations where different approaches can be taken to get the Red task done. If so, you may be able to adapt your approach to use your Greens, at least some. This is usually easier said than done, but many people like to advance this as a possibility to keep in mind.

Summarizing, these Six Guidelines are meant to encourage a person to allow sufficient time to do Red work, and once started, to complete it 75% of the time. It is a constant battle. The procrastination battle rages on and on. I hope these guidelines will help you win the battle from time to time!

CHAPTER SUMMARY

In this chapter I am suggesting a two-pronged, interrelated approach. *One*, that there are specific, concrete things we as responsible people can do to actually do Reds (rather than let them go), do them well and with the appropriate attitude while doing them.

Two, while not emphasized a lot in this chapter, but what I hope is a constant theme in this book, we can ask for God's help and strength before and while doing Reds. To me, simply asking for God's help will not work; just using the above Guidelines and Principles will not work either. It is both, not either or. Our goal is to literally please God while doing Greens <u>and</u> Reds. A tall order, but doable enabled by God's upholding strength.

SECTION TWO:

LIVING OUT YOUR CALLING AND DOING WHAT GOD DESIRES

CHAPTER 8
APPLICATION: JOB LIFE

The *goal* of this chapter is to think through issues and ramifications a person usually encounters in a Red job, Green job, and Yellow job, and in that order.

INTRODUCTION

In this chapter, we are considering only full-time jobs, not a part-time job or volunteer job. Full-time work usually means working 40 or so hours per week on the job. Granted, a person may work two or three part-time jobs that add up to 40 hours a week. While we will be considering only one full-time job, the concepts we will be dealing with can apply to a person having two or three jobs that add up to 40 or so hours weekly.

So in this chapter, we will look at three types of jobs—Red, Green, and Yellow jobs and also issues a person usually faces in these three types of jobs. And as we have said all along, we encourage people to be in Green work, rather than Yellow or Red work.

However, a person may find himself or herself in a Red job now, which a person should do temporarily, not long-term, as well as do this with his or her eyes wide open to its present and future ramifications on his or her life.

On the other hand, just because someone is in a "good" Green job now does not mean that particular job is for him or her now or in the future.

He or she must also be asking: "Does that job enable me to achieve my Life Purpose? Does it enable me to realize important Values?"

We should be making decisions in light of our Greens and Reds. As Charlene compared making job choices before and after knowing her Greens and Reds, she said: "If I don't know my Greens and Reds, it is a process of trial and error." Today she knows what direction she should be heading, in both job options and specific field. Presently she is taking educational courses to build up her knowledge needed for her Green chosen field. "I am excited now," she is saying. "I have hope. I am looking forward to seeing how God will continue leading me step by step."

While life is not a bed of roses, Charlene is doing her best to live out her Individual Calling . . . consistent with her Universal Calling. Her decisions have a God-centered focus, because she is devoted to God and understands more and more His Love for her. She admits: "Trusting God like this is new territory for me." Her future is unknown, but she knows in her heart God knows, and that is enough for her.

Compare Charlene's story with Fred's situation. He relates: "I have been in a Red job all my life. I hate cold canvassing and selling." He goes on: "What happened to me is (he is now 54) I did fairly well, at least compared to my work associates. I got awards, and lots of recognition. So while I hurt very badly inside, I stayed in sales and tried to hide my feelings. I landed a couple of big, lucrative accounts and with them, some large sales. It was more a fluke than my skills, but no one would believe me. I got so deeply into sales I felt I was in it too long and too deeply to pull out. And I didn't want to disappoint those who looked up to me."

Fred's story is a sad one. Apparent (outward) success cannot cover up real (inward) feelings. I encouraged Fred to reconsider, but he admitted his ego was his big stumbling block. In a hotel room with him and his wife, I asked him to "give himself up" and trust God like he has never done before. He broke down. His wife defended him, saying: "We can make it together to age 62, when Fred can retire."

He was living "distantly" from God. But the wonderful thing about God is that He will not abandon Fred or us or turn His face from us if we will but humble ourselves, confess, and seek Him. He will still hear our earnest prayers, even though presently we are not living in close/intimate relationship with Him. Isn't it interesting? When we need Him most, we are often living far from God.

Fred admitted as much. He said, "This job is eating me up. I have not seriously studied the Bible in years, and I go to church every Sunday, and have held several important church positions." We talked about the negative effects of a Red job on his walk with God. But Fred and his wife would not budge.

All said differently, Fred's identity was his job. His security was his job. I believe our identity is found in the person of Christ, not our jobs. Our jobs are very important, but a hundred thousand times more important is our Spiritual Life and walking as we know we should in the eyes of God, not primarily walking as others tell us we should be walking.

In God's eyes is Charlene successful? I believe so. Is Fred successful? Would you want to be in Fred's shoes now, five years from now, or at age 65? You must answer that question for yourself. This book is designed to help you avoid such situations. Personally, I would not want to be in his shoes.

With this Introduction, let's turn our attention to our three main subjects:

- a Red Job or
- a Green job or
- a Yellow job.

IN A RED JOB NOW

Assume the scenario of a person now in a Red job. The reasons for that are numerous; they include some unavoidable circumstances that forced him or her to give up a Green job and take a Red job. Or he or she has simply made wrong job choices (often caused by not knowing his or her Greens and Reds). Lots more reasons could be advanced.

But the fact remains he or she is there. His or her Job Satisfaction Indicator level is four or below. And because of that, his or her energy level is declining, enthusiasm ebbing, anger eruptions more frequent, and people seem to be irritating him or her more and more. These are typical ramifications of being in a Red job.

All said differently, someone in a Red job is out of his or her "Green zone," and wallowing deep in his or her "Red zone." Our Individual Call-

ing includes using our Greens and some of our Reds. That, along with all
the negative personal ramifications of being in Red work certainly justifies
one conclusion: change jobs.

As a first step, a person may try to change some of his or her responsibilities within his or her present job. Usually that is not enough. Often the
job he or she ends up with is at best Yellow, not Green. So that usually is
but half a solution.

So to state the obvious, the best solution is to change jobs, and look for a
Green job opportunity inside or outside his or her organization. Either way,
the "job" of looking for a new job is a Red for the vast majority of people,
besides a "thump" to one's ego. But keep the big picture in mind. What
does God desire? He created a person to experience job satisfaction— He
wants you to be satisfied in your toilsome work (Ecclesiastes 5:18-20), not
dissatisfied with work and life.

So embrace God; fill your thoughts and mind with His perspective;
brush off what others may tell you because they simply want to encourage
you during your down times. The truth of the matter is: if a person is in a
Red job, and no change is on the horizon, it will not get any better (some
encouragers may say things like "Oh, it will get better" or "Trust God more"
or "You can do it"). Instead, it will only get worse.

And to make matters even worse, a person tends to procrastinate getting
started in the job search, doing the job search itself, because "searching for
a job" is a Red for most people. But recall what we said about doing Reds
in Chapter 7. Is the Red simple or complex? For most people, the steps in
the search process are simple, hence doable.

Additionally, as also mentioned in Chapter 7, Plan Plus. Exercise lots of
discipline, AND remember, God will help you, if you will ask Him. But do
you trust Him? Ask only if you want His guidance and direction. He might
answer in ways you never dreamt of. Ephesians 3:20: "Now to him who is
able to do immeasurably more than all we ask or imagine, according to his
power that is at work within us."

HOW LONG IN A RED JOB?

People in Red jobs often ask me: "How long should a person stay in a
Red job?" Based on my studied observation of people for over 30 years, I
answer: "At the most, 18 months." Frankly I think that is stretching it a

bit; the By-Products of Red work (fig. 2-b) usually appear strong and hard sooner.

See if this is not what usually happens. If someone starts a Red job, he or she usually does not really know if it is a Green or Red because he or she has not discovered his or her Greens and Reds. But he or she hopes it will be a good and satisfying job.

He or she initially feels excited about the new job, new people, the hours, etc. The first three months usually go just fine. But if it is a Red job, during the first three to six months, the initial interest in and excitement for the job starts waning. Then there is the "thump"—the realization he or she really does not like the work.

With this scenario in mind, I reiterate that staying in a Red job as long as 18 months may be a stretch. As noted earlier, there may be overriding factors that justify more than 18 months, but I stress, do this knowingly, aware of the serious negative ramifications of Red work on a person's attitude, energy level, etc.

ONCE AGAIN . . . YOUR WALK WITH GOD

At the end of Chapter 2, among three benefits to a person from knowing his or her Greens and Reds was "the impact of Greens and Reds on relationships." And not only our horizontal (other people) relationships, but also our vertical (with God) relationship. As we said in Chapter 2: a person in Red work tends to have less (or little) potential for a close/intimate walk with God, whereas someone in Green work has more (or greater) potential for a close/intimate walk with God.

I have asked scores of people whose Job Satisfaction Indicator level is 4 or less (10 high, 5 average, 1 low) these questions: "How are you doing spiritually? Are you walking closely with God? Has your relationship with God lost its intimacy?" Then they give me this increasingly painful look.

Everyone replies this way: "It is really rough now . . . I am down spiritually . . . reading the Bible is so ho-hum . . . I feel like a robot reading it. Something is wrong, but I can't put a finger on it." And this is said by people from all walks of life—those making big and small salaries, people working in Christian or secular vocations—everyone. Low job satisfaction is a merciless leveler.

A company president called me to "do my thing" at his company employing 250 people. After identifying his Greens and Reds, and following up with him that included doing the Job Match-up exercise (Chapter 5), the conclusion was clear: he was in a Red job.

During my feedback conference with him, I gave him the "Red news" and with that, two options that would be Green jobs for him. As I was leaving his office, he said to me at the door in a hushed voice: "I hate this job, but I have never told that to anyone. I feel a huge burden has been lifted from my shoulders this past 30 minutes."

Two days later I did further follow up with him, including asking about his spiritual life. He said "It is far from what it should be.... I feel distant from God . . . I wish I knew what was causing it." When I told him that perhaps his low job satisfaction was contributing to his spiritual doldrums, his eyes lit up and you could see the wheels turning in his mind. You see, previously he told me how he was trying to exercise all kinds of discipline to refresh his spiritual life, including a secluded weekend of fasting at a conference retreat facility. Nothing worked.

In the face of being viewed "out of his mind" by his friends and work associates, he hired another person to replace him as president; meanwhile, he took a staff position for his company that put him into a Green job.

Ideal? Yes. Practical? Yes. Spiritually life-saving? I believe so. Repeating: ANYTHING THAT INTERFERES WITH A PERSON HAVING A CLOSE WALK WITH GOD IS THEIR ENEMY. I underscore anything. I realize there are other significant causes for people getting off track with God. But low job satisfaction is often an overlooked culprit in the search for reasons a person is drooping spiritually.

This company president made a bold, God-pleasing decision. His walk with God is a Spiritual Value. He is not just "talking the talk" but he is "walking the walk." While there is no earthly applause for his decision, I have a strong suspicion there was "heavenly applause."

WHY PEOPLE STAY IN RED JOBS (ESPECIALLY HIGH-PAYING RED JOBS)

Red jobs usually negatively impact life at every turn . . . at home, church, and on the job. In spite of these negative life ramifications, why do some people intentionally stay in Red jobs (including jobs that pay well)? Here are four (and there are more) reasons people have shared with well-intentioned, well-meaning hearts. You can judge their validity for yourself.

Reason one—I want to <u>provide well</u> for my family.

No one can dispute this goal of providing well for family; it is a right thing to do. The Bible encourages a believer to provide for relatives and family. (See 1 Timothy 5:8) But I often see people going overboard in this "providing well" business. It often means one or both of two things. One, having the wherewithal to live in an unnecessarily large house and two, providing for all or most of their kid's college education. And to do these, they need a high income; they then "do what it takes." Often this means doing Red work.

You already know how I feel about shooting for a dream/big house that requires parents to work in their Reds because those jobs pay well. Then add onto that the added burden and stress when parents think it is their responsibility primarily to fund their children's education . . . and that might include some private pre-college school as well as college.

Repeating, it is a laudable goal to want to help one's children in any way possible. But there are limits, too. Frankly, I never felt that was a primary parental responsibility. Our children completed college; we contributed as best we could to their education, but my wife and I never felt the weight of paying the entire freight. Nor, in fact, did we even insist they go to college; it was their choice.

In my view, parents should deliberately think through their ideas and thoughts about funding their children's education. Here are a couple questions I ask as food for thought:

1. What do you think kids prefer . . . a parent who comes home having worked in his or her Greens all day, or in Reds all day?
2. Do you think kids prefer parents who are walking closely with God, or distantly from God? You and I know what answer would please God.

Then I add: there is nothing unspiritual about asking teenagers to work a year or two after they graduate from high school. There is nothing wrong with a college student stretching out or extending his or her time in college another year or two and work part-time.

So what is more important for a parent? To be in a position to "fund everything" and not be the kind of Christian you know in your heart you want to be and should be? Or "fund partially" and do your best to be the kind of Christian you know in your heart you should be? So parents need to think through what it means to provide well for their family. Perhaps a statement like: "I want to provide adequately for my family" would be both more realistic and less stress producing.

We always need to keep things in perspective and balance, and that includes what it means to be responsible family providers. Our role is not to "keep up with the Jones." Instead, our role is to keep our decisions under God's microscope, not under the "what others do" microscope. In my view, long-term Red work is a recipe for disaster, even if it means financial success.

Reason two: That God is pleased when a person <u>hates</u> his work.

You will be surprised how many people believe God in fact desires that people hate their work. When I first heard this I thought people were kidding (that did not win any points with them!). But they were dead serious.

Simplistically stated, their "rationale" goes like this. Things would be too easy if we liked our work since it would require little, if any, self-discipline and sacrifice. Therefore, a person should hate his or her work. In turn, this would then force him or her on a daily basis to exercise lots and lots of self-discipline, as well as keep him or her "humble" and self-sacrificing.

In turn, such severe self-discipline would develop character, and also cause a person to trust God in ways he or she never had to do previously. All this sounds good, even Scriptural. But life is trying and difficult enough without the smothering effects of a Red job.

Reiterating: a person in a Green job, with a goal of being God's ambassador there, will be tested and challenged to the hilt at every turn. It requires self-discipline and sacrifice. Any workplace can be a jungle of temptations, and moral and ethical challenges.

So a person need not resort to self-mutilizing techniques, like "I must hate my work," to be tested and so develop character, etc. Sometimes I feel people who think this way do not want to be responsible for their actions and performance or want to know their Greens and Reds, because if they did, it might require some big changes in their life and lifestyles.

Reason three: It is _selfish_ for a person to want job satisfaction; besides that, it is a _self-serving_ concept.

In my view, nothing could be further from the truth than to say only selfish people want job satisfaction and that it is a self-serving concept. It is interesting what people in Red work (especially high-paying jobs) come up with!

Of course, we know from Ecclesiastes 5:18-20 that the concept of job satisfaction is a Biblical concept. It is surprising how few people have noticed this Scripture. Setting aside the fact they may be unaware of Scripture's teaching on this matter, I believe many people say it is selfish to want job satisfaction because they are "locked in" or do not want to make a change. They may be locked in by "good benefits," short commute, unwilling to change their lifestyles or, yes, even change their thinking.

I try explaining to people that satisfaction is a means, a means for pleasing God, not the end. Then some people say: "I don't want satisfaction to be my god." Well, neither do I want it to be my god. But there should be little danger of satisfaction being self-serving or a god when our motives are to glorify God (Universal Calling) and please Him. Green work and being fruitful (being Christian) go hand in hand. Red work and being touchy and grumpy (not being Christian) a lot go hand in hand. God created us to be satisfied, not dissatisfied, all the time. Put another way, only people satisfied in their work have the potential, with God's help, to be unselfish and serving ambassadors for Jesus.

Reason four: I want to be a _stay-at-home_ parent

The job of stay-at-home parent may be the most important job in the world. In my mind, there is no more important supervisory job in the world than parenting. Kids need their parents. It is so great to hear parents saying they want to be with their kids. But what if parenting is a Red for someone? Here again, we need to deal with the issues and ramifications of being in Red work with eyes wide open.

Parenting and homemaking is a Red for many people. For example, it is a total Red for Strategy people; it is also Red for at least three-quarters of Ideas people. Fewer people are in their Reds parenting and homemaking if they are Relationships or Tasks people.

Look in on Maureen, a Red-working stay-at-home parent with three kids. She is a deeply committed believer. She loves her husband and kids. Her husband has a good job; they just bought their first house. "I do not like being a homemaker," she is saying, "I can't stand being everyone's slave." Then she asked: "What should a person do when homemaking is a 'have to', not 'want to'?" She does not want to leave them in day care all day long.

Here is the solution we worked out. First, we identified her Greens and Reds. And as you would expect, she did not list taking care of the kids as a Positive Experience. In this process, you could see the false guilt rising from her as we determined that parenting was her Red. Now she understood the reason for feeling the way she does towards parenting; and that it was not her, per se, but that she was functioning in her Reds.

My recommendation to anyone in this situation (in a Red job) is to get some Green into his or life. This usually means suggesting he or she does something Green for at least five hours weekly—yes, to bring not only some Green into his or her life, but also to give him or her something to look forward to each week, or a little Green hope in the midst of his or her lots-of-Reds life.

What the person actually does those five or more hours weekly may or may not be for compensation. The important issue here is to get some Green into their life while respecting Maureen's desire to remain at home.

Maureen located a Green eight-hours-a-week (two mornings) job. She and her husband hired someone to care for the kids at their home. Her husband is thrilled. Maureen is thrilled. In fact, she now feels better about homemaking, and her husband has seen an upswing in her attitude.

Is this a perfect solution? No, but in this case and cases like it, half a loaf (some Green) is better than none (no Green). Decisions are being made with eyes wide open—open to the fact of Maureen's Greens and Reds. Maureen and her husband are working things out in a practical, workable manner. Applause, please, for their willingness to make the adjustments in their thinking and weekly schedules!

A mini-summary: These are but some of the reasons people stay in Red work. Some you may agree with, others disagree. But recall: the biggest reason among all the reasons advanced for a person being in Green work is that he or she then has the potential for an intimate walk with God.

On the other hand, Red work reduces that possibility . . . in my opinion, a lot. How does God view success? One way is that we view God Himself and the resources we have in Jesus and the Holy Spirit sufficient. "The Lord is my Shepherd, I shall not want" (Psalm 23). Our "means" to Him is our relationship with Him. Sheep "listen to his voice" (John 10:3). Sheep that are walking not close to God may not hear God's still small voice. Think about it.

So extenuating circumstances may keep someone in Red work for extended periods of time. But these should be the exception rather than the rule. Look at success from God's standpoint. He wants to walk closely with you. Can He? Is He?

IN A GREEN JOB NOW

Let us switch gears now and talk about people in a Green job. It is refreshing to function with people in Green work, desiring nothing more. I often ask them what their Job Heart Desires/aspirations are, or "In your heart of hearts, what is it that you want to do?"

Almost apologetically they say: "All I want is to do my best where I am now. I am so fortunate." As soon as I hear something like that, in my eyes, their maturity and credibility skyrocket. I immediately say to them: "You are a mature person."

In my view, here is someone working hard, living Christianly, and desiring nothing more job-wise than to do what is in front of him or her. He or she is not being sidetracked by externally imposed desires like "move up the ladder" or "you deserve to be paid more money," and the like. His or her desire is to "impress" God (really please God), not impress people.

Some people may accuse such a person of not having ambition. Instead, I would say he or she has lots of ambition . . . ambition that is God-centered, not this world-centered. And he or she is most apt to be having a close, quiet, intimate walk with God. He or she values most a relationship with God, not primarily some "position" or impressive title (all of which is temporary anyway, 2 Corinthians 4:18).

IN A <u>LOW-PAYING</u> FIELD AND GREEN JOB

We all know some fields pay a lot less than others. Generally speaking, a staff worker in a retirement facility can expect to make less money than someone selling real estate. A social worker can usually expect to make less money than someone designing diesel engines for a manufacturer. A nanny can expect to make less now and in the future than a physician.

Let us assume a person is working in his or her Greens, achieving her Life Purpose—helping the people he or she believes would please God, and realizing key Values in his or her life. But he or she is barely scraping by financially and is on a tight budget, watching every nickel being spent.

The question is: should he or she stay in Green work (and a low paying field) or jump into a different field/occupation that pays more (assuming he or she could do that) but would pull him or her away from his or her primary areas of interest as well as his or her Greens.

While you may feel differently, if any person believes what he or she is doing now is pleasing God (so living out his or her Individual Calling), I usually recommend this person remain where he or she is, even though the income potential is comparatively low; and continue adjusting his or her lifestyle consistent with the income. Yes, yes, I know this is easier said than done. But we are back to the question: How does God view your success?

In 1976, my first year in this business, I made $7,200, the next few years were also 'lean'. The way I have operated this business has meant comparatively low income to us (our family); it is still this way.

Have we had to tighten our belts? You bet. Scrimped? Yes, yes. Have we had life's necessities. Yes, oh yes. Am I sorry for what we could not purchase for our kids? No. Should we have done more, according to today's world's standards? Yes.

Has God been faithful? Yes, a thousand million times over. Have we consistently tried to embrace our Christian Values and Priorities? Well, I know we have tried our best. As I look back, would I trade it in for a job that paid better? No, we have no regrets. I would not trade being able to spend time studying God's Word and praying for those I believe I should for all the "tea in China."

Am I a success in this business from this world's viewpoint? Financially, no. But we did survive (!) 30 plus years. Have we experienced times of stress (especially when no income is coming in)? Yes. Have I thought of getting out of the business? With tongue-in-cheek I say: "Once a week, at least." Never seriously, but it can and does get discouraging at times (like any job).

I tell you about these things because it is my view each family, each person should be willing to make adjustments in their lifestyle and spending habits. I have often said somewhat facetiously, but there is an element of truth to it: "If you do not have the money, there are not any decisions to make"—decisions like whether or not you should get a bigger home, or another car, etc.

The key to being in a low-paying field (and in our Greens) is contentment and not looking at what other people do out of the corner of your eye, comparing what they do or have with what you do not have or are not doing. Satan gets into thoughts and before we know it, he has you thinking you are a person to be pitied, rather than someone who is the recipient of God's gracious grace and love.

As I look back now, I cannot explain how we did it. I literally believe God carried us. How? I don't know. When? I don't know. I don't need to "figure out" God and how He works. This is His business, not my business. My role is to believe God is God, period and trust Him (John 14:1). It is pretty humbling to sit at this monitor and realize what I am saying to you. Our family is indeed a rich and richly blessed family.

IN A <u>HIGH-PAYING</u> FIELD AND GREEN JOB

Let's turn the tables from low-paying to high-paying scenarios and ask: Should a person stay in a high-paying Green job? The answer is not an automatic "yes." The person still needs to ask questions like: Am I achieving my Life Purpose now? Am I realizing my Values and Priorities now? Is my/our lifestyle "crazy" or rational now? And very importantly, is the person walking closely with God now? I emphasize NOW in each of these questions. Someday may never happen.

Well-to-do people have a huge responsibility before God and what it means for them personally to be responsible stewards of all GOD is enabling them to have. There is nothing more beautiful than a person who "has a ton of money," but you would never know it talking to them. You know they are walking closely with Jesus.

So if someone is in a high-paying Green job and living as he or she knows he or she should in the eyes of God, he or she should stay there. But if that job is "eating him or her up" or pulling him or her away from God, then I ask, "Is it worth it? Even temporarily worth it?"

Among many other things, walking closely with God requires time and discipline. I believe one of the keys opening the door for close fellowship with God is having time alone with God periodically—time for personal Bible reading/study, reflection, meditating on God, and praying for people God has placed on their hearts.

I now have seven 3 x 5 cards filled with names of people for whom I pray. I believe prayer is THE work of all believers . . . and frankly, lots of times prayer is just that—work. Some weeks I meet my goal of "time alone with God" five days out of seven. Other times I only do that two or three times. But I refuse to give up . . . instead I keep my goal in front of me and do my best to be consistent.

I like praying for people, I seldom tell them I am praying for them. That is between God and me. Are my prayers effective? I have no idea. Do I pray the right way? I don't know. What I do know is that my role is to pray with a pure heart and pure motives, and not be concerned primarily about how effective I am. There may be two, twenty, or two hundred people praying for someone, so who am I to make prayer evaluations? We walk by faith, not sight (2 Corinthians 5:7). By faith, I believe God is pleased when I study His Word and pray. That is good enough for me.

God is the Source, the Giver, the Master Provider. My wife and I consider ourselves rich people . . . not as rich financially as some people, richer financially than other people. When you and I compare what we have with poverty-stricken people, WE ARE RICH. We all have the sacred responsibility to be responsible and grateful stewards of our resources, large or little.

So if we have enough food, shelter, and clothing, we are very rich. "But if we have food and clothing, we will be content with that" (1 Timothy 6:8). We ALL need to heed the admonishment of Matthew 19:24: ". . . It is easier for a camel to go through the eye of a needle than for a rich man to enter the kingdom of God." Have you ever thought through and applied that verse to yourself?

God's Individual Calling is to all people. He desires that His people receive job satisfaction. Some jobs pay more than others. The key issue is not how much a person makes financially, but how much a person is abiding in Christ (John 15). Are you?

IN A YELLOW JOB NOW

We have been considering Red job and Green job scenarios. One remains—someone now in a Yellow job. Recall we said someone is in a Yellow job when his or her Job Satisfaction Indicator (1-low, 5-average, 10-high) level is between 4 and 6. As we mentioned in Chapter 5, this usually means his or her job life is like a roller coaster, up and down. Some days he or she is up—energized, excited; other days down—no energy, no excitement, no zip.

All things being equal, we can say one thing for sure: a Yellow job is better than a Red job, but it cannot hold a candle to a Green job. So should a person stay in a Yellow job permanently, regardless of income (but especially if it pays well)? I discourage it because of its detrimental effect on one's walk with God. So even if a person is achieving his or her Life Purpose and realizing his or her Values and Priorities (while in Yellow work), it is risky business to remain there. Plus, it is too hit-or-miss . . . the "down" days happen in every job, including Green jobs. Recall we said there is no perfect job (all Greens). But in my view, there are just too many down days in Yellow work. Why? Not enough satisfaction from the work to be consistent with Ecclesiastes 3:18-20's instructions to "find satisfaction in our toilsome work."

In a nutshell, I do not believe God's Individual Calling is to function permanently in a Yellow job, especially a Yellow job with no possibility to change the job to include more Greens. God's call is for us to use the Greens He gave us; He is pleased when a person looks for and finds Green work.

A YELLOW JOB "SOLUTION"

For the sake of argument, let us say a person, for very good reasons (and God-pleasing reasons, not rationalizations), feels he or she should stay in his or her Yellow job for the foreseeable future. Now this scenario takes nothing away from what I have said previously and that I believe God's call is to Green work for everyone. But let's "open the door" to the once-in-a-while possibility that a person really cannot change his or her job. He or she is stuck in a Yellow job. What should he or she do?

One solution (or at least a partial help) is for him or her to do something Green-for-them either part-time or as a volunteer someplace. By so doing, he or she can perhaps "Green up" his or her life a bit . . . perhaps move his or her overall job satisfaction (Yellow full-time job and Green part-time job) level from say 5 to 6 or 7. This way he or she is at least bordering on Green.

But, of course, this should be done with eyes wide open (we have heard that before!) That is, open to the possibility that the two jobs will be all time-consuming, thus resulting in other important Values-Priorities going unrealized—values like family time, time alone with God, taking care of aged parents, and the like. So this "solution" has a serious down side. In my view, not a very good answer to the Yellow job problem/issue, but at least it addresses the issue in hopes of upping a person's level of job satisfaction.

The other side is: never, never take a Red job (as a volunteer or part-time) while in a Yellow job. Why? It will tip the balance the other way, moving your overall job satisfaction downward from say 5 to 4 or 3. In other words, you go from a Yellow job to an overall Red or bordering-on-Red job.

Isn't it interesting? As I am writing this, a client called who is now in a Yellow job. This person said: "The longer I am in this job, the more frustrated I am becoming. I think it is beginning to turn Red. When I get home at night, I am frazzled and pooped . . . I have no energy for anything else."

He called for my advice. I said: "Go back to the drawing board. Ask yourself: 'In your heart of hearts, what do you really want to do?' Revisit your Positive Experiences Listing. Think through your Life Purpose and who you want to be helping."

At the end of our conversation I asked: "How are you doing spiritually?" "Awful, just awful," was his reply. He knew what he should be doing but did not have the "fuel"—job satisfaction to get him there.

Life is complex. But throw into the mix a person having to do either Red or Yellow work, and life gets almost unbearable. I urge you to take Scripture seriously. View God with fear and reverence. Tip your heart so it is receptive to God "Sprinkling Down" His Holy Spirit into your mind, emotions, and will. ". . . For you, LORD, have never forsaken those who seek you" (Psalm 9:10b).

CHAPTER SUMMARY

In this chapter, we have raised issues and questions to help a person think through three kinds of job situations: Red, Green, and Yellow. For most of us, job is important because that is where we will spend the majority of our time. That is reality. As such, we should be responsible Christians doing our best right now in light of our Greens and Reds.

The ramifications of Red work are too serious to be ignored. Yellow work is, like a roller coaster, a dangerous ride. In the long run, the only good answer is Green work that gives you the potential to be an Enoch Christian. "Enoch walked with God" (Genesis 5:24a). "For before he (Enoch) was taken [into heaven], he was commended as one who pleased God" (Hebrews 11:5b). No plaques, no books written, no offices held. Nothing, except it pleased God that he walked with Him. Are you?

THREE TIDBITS

I really did not know where to include the following three tidbits. I run into these three situations often in my work; perhaps they might be instructive to you. The first one is a sad story about someone in his Reds, the second a question about starting one's own business, the third about working long hours. One or two of them may interest you. If not, Chapter 9 awaits you.

1: The Charles "Ramifications of Reds" Story

Charles has moved up the ladder while making three major job changes the past eight years. Each change meant considerably more money, desirable titles, and also more traveling. Ten years ago, we had pinpointed his Greens and Reds.

"Why am I so miserable all the time?" Charles asked me. I asked him what his present level of job satisfaction was. He answered, "Two to three." The cause for his "miserableness" was job mismatch . . . his job responsibilities did not match up with his Greens and other strengths.

"Where did I go wrong?" he asked. "I sought out people I trusted for counsel and advice."

"Did you take into account your Greens and Reds when you made those job changes?" I asked. "No," was his reply.

"And why didn't you call me when you were making those changes? We could have done the job match-up exercise in two minutes on the telephone?"

"I didn't call you because I was afraid of what you would tell me. Besides, I believed I could change a Red into a Green, and that by hard work, discipline, training, plus enough experience, that I could cut it. And too, all my advisors said go for it. At the time, making more money seemed like the responsible thing to do. And it was enticing . . . a new job, new title, and a prestigious position. It just seemed like the right thing to do at the time."

"Did anyone at any time ask you what your skills were," I asked, "Or what gave you job satisfaction?"

"Not one" was his sheepish reply.

Here is the point. It is your responsibility to take into account your Greens and Reds when making job choices; do not count on others to help you do it. Most other people do not think in terms of Greens and Reds.

And we all like encouragement, but "go for it" encouragement will not change the fact of your Greens and Reds. Do not ignore what you know to be your Greens and Reds. Do not end up like Charles . . . miserable, when with a little forethought, he could have avoided a lot of misery. AND Charles admitted to not having a good time alone with God in four or five years.

2: Should I start my own business?

I am often asked: "Should I start my own business?" I am not expert in business startups. The library and other resources are jammed with information on this subject. But I am often asked this question after identifying someone's Greens and Reds.

Here is my usual answer. First and foremost . . . make sure what you will be doing day-in, day-out lands you smack in the middle of your Greens. If not, raise a Red flag and raise it high! So if designing is a person's Green, then that person may consider starting a design business. If teaching is a person's Green, go into a business enabling them to teach. If cleaning and organizing physical space or buildings is someone's Green, go into that type business.

Now many people may tell you marketing is the key to a successful business. Marketing is important to many businesses, but I believe right alongside of that in importance is that a person is doing Green work. Often this is not taken into account in the should-I-start-my-own-business decision process.

Two more tidbits I pass along to people. One, if possible try out the business part-time (while employed) before going full-time. Two, keep non-controllable expenses down, especially at the start. A non-controllable expense is one you cannot control once you decide to do it . . . it is due every week or month . . . you cannot control it, only pay it. Examples include monthly rent, utilities, loan payments, and the like.

As a general rule, I have my "Hagstrom Laws"—two of them. They keep my feet on the ground; they are the way things happen.

Law one: it always costs more. Law two: it always takes longer. Buy a computer and soon it is costing more than you originally thought, with updates, new software, and the like. My major point is that it will cost more than you think to start and run a business, and take longer to get it to the point of it being "up and running." These two laws apply to almost any project we undertake from starting a business, renovating a room, or writing a book!

3—Over-Extension

Over-extension is a concept that applies to the total amount of time a person spends each week on the job. Every time I ask individuals or groups to describe today's lifestyle, the most descriptive words are: "It is a hassle." Or they use words like

- fractured
- go-go-go
- always in a hurry
- no time to think
- always meeting some schedule or appointment.

I wonder what God thinks of this kind of lifestyle? Do you think God is calling you to live this way?

In my view, one reason (among many) we get into the "it is a hassle bind" is what I call Over-extension. Over-extension means working on the job too many hours. Someone over-extending is usually working around 60 hours plus weekly, including commute time. Sure, there are busy times when we all have to go beyond 60 hours, but this should be the exception, not the rule.

Over-extended people need to ask themselves some serious questions. Among such questions are: Should I modify my definition of job success? What Values Priorities are going unrealized? What impact is this having on significant relationships in my life, and on my day-in, day-out walk with God? Is my job "eating me up" so that I have little or no time to reach out to others with needs as a volunteer?

In Chapter 10, we will describe another cause for over-extension: too many volunteer jobs at one time.

CHAPTER 9
APPLICATION: THE CARRY-OVER PRINCIPLE AND HOME LIFE

The *goal* of the *next two chapters* is to point out how our jobs often affect our attitude, relationships, and action (or lack thereof) at home or while serving as a volunteer (e.g. at church, or a community organization). So if a job takes a total of 10 or so hours daily, we will point out how that job may impact the six or so remaining waking hours of the day.

The *goal* of *this chapter* is to zero in on our home life, and how our jobs may either positively or negatively affect how we act in our homes.

INTRODUCTION

Gail comes home from work tired, but upbeat and positive. Rachael comes home from work tired, but dragging it . . . dog tired . . . too pooped to pop, as they say. George comes home from work tired, but upbeat and positive. Ralph comes home from work tired, but dragging it . . . dog tired, too pooped to pop, as they say.

Thinking now only of your home life, whom would you rather live with? Whom would you rather be? Or which person would you rather be faced with the task of making a meal? Or the job of mowing the lawns? Or having to drive the kids to a soccer game or giving tired kids a bath? Or having to clean and tidy up the house for weekend guests? Or "downing a bite to eat," then jumping in the car to go grocery shopping . . . or sitting at the kitchen table and paying the bills? Not to mention the possibility of going to choir practice, or a committee meeting, or a family birthday party on the other side of town?

I am sure the answer is obvious to you. You would rather be the person whose name begins with G, coming home tired but upbeat. And you would rather live with such a person. The other side is: you would rather not be the person whose name begins with R who comes home "dragging it." Nor would it be a "church picnic" living with him or her.

The G-people are in Green jobs at work (including stay-at-home parents). That is, their responsibilities match up well with their Greens, so they are getting lots of satisfaction from their work. The R-people are in Red jobs at work; their responsibilities do not match up with their Greens so they are getting virtually no satisfaction from their work. Granted, both are tired when they get home, but there is a Green tired and a Red tired. A Green tired is not debilitating; in their tiredness, they are still upbeat and positive. A Red tired is debilitating in the sense that they are emotionally and physically down . . . exhausted and often very discouraged.

Certainly someone in Green work can come home down and discouraged from time to time; even then, with God's help, a person in Green work has the potential to handle it better than someone in Red work.

THE CARRY-OVER PRINCIPLE

Here is the major point of the Introduction illustrations. Our jobs and the level of job satisfaction (or lack thereof) **carries over** into and greatly affects our off-the-job life—at home, at church, at the grocery store, and the like. I call this the Carry-Over Principle.

In Chapter 6, the Spill Over Concept was described. There we saw how the satisfaction (fuel) from doing Greens could be drawn upon to help us do the Reds in our jobs. Similarly, as Green fuel energizes us to do Greens and some Reds on the job, so a Green job can have positive effects on our off-the-job life, both at home and at church (as a volunteer, the subject of the next chapter).

Look at fig. 9-a, "Carry-Over." This summarizes how Green work (full-time) and Red work (full-time) affects a person's Attitudes, Relationships, and Action when they walk through the door, coming home from another day's work. And if being a stay-at-home parent is someone's full-time work, the Carry-Over principle still applies . . . except such a person may want to walk out the door after a day's work of taking care of two or three young-sters (just kidding, just kidding!).

In a nutshell, and said simplistically, Green work (full-time) tends to have a positive effect on life off-the-job, Red work tends to have a negative effect on life off-the-job. Of course, as we indicated in Chapter 8, Over-extension (working/commuting too long . . . over 60 hours weekly) can also raise havoc with a responsible lifestyle.

I hope from the bottom of my heart that you understand why it is so important to be in a Green job. Two reasons include wanting to be a positive influence both at work and home, but also be a cooperative, "how can I help you" person there AND at home. That is a tall order. The Carry-Over effect of Green work has the potential to impact one's home life positively.

Reiterating . . . our Individual Calling is to please God. One way we do this is by using our Greens and some of our Reds. The satisfaction or sense of accomplishment we get from doing Greens is usually a significant energy source fueling our desires and goals, and putting feet under our Values (e.g. being a loving parent, or caring spouse).

BUSY, BUSY . . . ACTIVITY, ACTIVITY

Aah, but if life were only simpler, less complicated. Would it not be nice to know if someone is in a Green job, then life at home would be a "bed of roses"—calm, restful, relaxing, and edifying? But life at home is usually anything but that.

Sometimes parents do not know whether to be yesterday's enforcer or today's encourager. Or both. Tensions (often unspoken), conflict, loud voices (and TV noise) are often the rule, rather than the exception. Sooner or later we come to our senses and realize we have not been the godly people we want to be, even strongly desire to be.

Psalm 101:2 (Living Bible) says it well: "I will try to walk a blameless path, but how I need your help, especially in my own home, where I long to act as I should." I believe the author of deception, Satan, is ALWAYS lurk-ing in the cupboards and underneath couch cushions ready to pounce at the moment we think we can "let down" at home. Did I hear someone say being Christian is always testing? Yes, home is a testing ground.

CARRY-OVER

A. How a full-time job (Green or Red) may carry over into and affect life off the job, e.g. home life, church life, community life, etc.

Green Work (full-time)	Red Work (full-time)
Satisfied	Dissatisfied
Do well (A, B+)	Not do well (D+, C)

CARRY-OVER From Green Work	CARRY OVER From Red Work
Most potential to be…	Most potential to be…
ATTITUDES	ATTITUDES
1. Positive	1. Negative
2. Cooperative	2. Less willing, reluctant
RELATIONSHIPS	RELATIONSHIPS
3. (Have) positive relationships (Have) best people skills	3. (Have) negative relationships (Have) not-so-good people skills
ACTION	ACTION
4. Helping doer	4. Reluctant doer
5. Self-starter	5. Procrastinator

fig. 9-a

B. How the off-the-job responsibility itself, whether Green or Red, may affect someone's <u>willingness</u> to do it.

   1. If now in Green work (full-time), he will tend to be most willing to do Green (off-the-job) things and <u>somewhat willing</u> to do Red things.

   2. If now in Red work (full-time), he <u>may be willing</u> to do Green things (remember, he comes home both pooped and "down") and usually <u>very, very reluctant</u> (often unwilling) to do Red things.

Note: At no point is it suggested or implied a person should not do Red-for-them "stuff" when that is essential to do.

fig. 9-a(2)

In light of our desire to "walk a blameless path" (Psalm 101:2) and the reality of how life usually really is at home, I have struggled thinking about how to approach living out our calling during Home Life. Hundreds of excellent books have been written on how to be a good parent, or be a good spouse, or how to build Christian homes, and the like. I do not want to duplicate such writings.

In conversations with other people, coupled with my own views, we all seem to agree on two things.

- One, life itself is complex and testing every day
- Two, life at home is equally, if not more complex and testing. It may be less difficult being Christian on a two-week short-term mission trip, than to be consistently Christian in one's own home.

This being so, we must not lose heart. God is still God, and the Bible is still God's Word to us right now. His Holy Spirit is always available to counsel, enable, and empower (see again Luke 11:13 about asking for His Holy Spirit). Individually, we must believe and act responsibly. God greatly desires that we please and glorify Him at home. In light of this, let us look at Home Life two ways. First, let us take a closer look at our Attitudes, Relationships, and Actions (from fig. 9-a). Second, doing a job match-up will help you find out what at-home responsibilities may be Green or Red.

HOME LIFE . . . ATTITUDE

Some people say: "Attitude is everything." I hope they do not mean everything in the sense that there is nothing else important. Instead, I hope and think it means that attitude is basic, foundational, spilling over into everything—our thoughts, words, and actions. Sour attitude, sour person. Negative attitude, negative person . . . everything and everyone is wrong. Pessimism rules our lives with this kind of attitude.

On the other hand, someone with a positive attitude can see the good in a person or situation. He or she can reason objectively, compared to someone who is negative. While facing difficulties, he or she still has hope. He or she tends to be optimistic, not pessimistic.

No one is always negative or always positive. When things seem to go wrong, it is easy to get negative. When kids disobey, it is not a cause for rejoicing. When your spouse seems to contradict or question your every word, it is easy to seethe inside or pop off, or sulk.

If attitude is basic and foundational, affecting our thoughts, words, and actions (even loud ones . . . stomping feet!), what are we to do? To whom are we to look?

While it may seem like a "I tried it once and failed" or "That is not possible in my situation" issue, I would strongly urge you to consider Jesus' attitude. This should be our attitude standard, even if we feel we will only partially attain it. By the way, I believe if we lower the bar to something less than Jesus' perfect attitude, we leave the door wide open to being less than God wants, as well as reducing our chances of growing in our attitude.

Jesus came to serve. ". . . Just as the Son of Man did not come to be served, but to serve . . ." (Matthew 20:28). His example is our model. Jesus is always our only model; people are never our models. Is God pleased and glorified when we strive to do things with the right attitude—a serving heart? Even when our spouse irritates us? Or the kids disobey? Personally, my big, ongoing, always-difficult test or challenge is this business of consistently having a "here to serve you" attitude.

Frankly, I find myself getting irritated if people bring it up too much. Why? Their comments "stab me in the heart." They always bring it up when I have a poor attitude. This is tough territory, easy to talk about, but in my opinion one of the most difficult things to do consistently day-in, day-out . . . "especially in my own home where I long to act as I should."

Then the Apostle Paul had the "audacity" to write: "Submit to one another out of reverence to Christ" (Ephesians 5:21). Out of reverence to Christ? Yes, I am to submit to others because I reverence Christ in my heart. Why doesn't Scripture say to do this anywhere but home?

In a nutshell, if Christ's life means anything to me, I am to be in awe of Him, deeply respecting Him and loving Him (reverencing Christ, Ephesians 5:21). I live that out by serving others and submitting (mutual submission—"to one another," Ephesians 5:21) in the sense of listening to others correction and/or learning from them.

So our attitude at home, like everywhere else, should be one of being willing to serve at the drop of a hat. Saying no to that first impulse to serve often proves fatal to walking "the serving-others walk." Satan wants us to say no. Instead, we should be listening to Jesus' tender, beckoning Voice that says yes to serving others . . . and doing that right now, not tomorrow.

In a Green Job Now

Look again at fig. 9-a. Notice that someone in a Green job has the *potential* for the right attitude. Why potential? First, it is never (for me at least) easy to do. Second, there is the pride factor. Let us consider each one.

First, why is it never easy to have a consistent "serving others" attitude? Why does it always seem to be a struggle point? For each of us, we hate giving up OUR RIGHTS. This seems to get harder to do the older I get. It requires me to pick up my cross daily and voluntarily (Luke 9:23). Also notice the little word "if" which implies I have a choice—I don't have to do it.

"If [you can say no, but then you would not be His disciple] anyone [you, them, and I] would come after me, he must deny himself [ugh!] and take up his cross daily [why not once a month!] and follow me" Luke 9:23.

By denying myself (giving up MY rights), with Christ's help I have the opportunity to follow him—even follow him through the back door of our house and into the kitchen. It is an opportunity, not "take away" from what you might really want to do. It is an opportunity to be the bearer of unity, harmony, and a lot less conflict. It is an opportunity to serve, without going 5,000 miles to a mission field. Our mission field includes our homes.

So as we drive into the driveway or climb the stairs to the apartment, we are soon in opportunity land—home. As the door swings open, a person has the potential for the right attitude (Exhibit A, fig. 9-a). As you are "hit with a problem" or told about a wonderful day someone had, you have the opportunity to care about them OR care more about your schedule and what you want to do. At that instant, your reaction reveals your true attitude. It happens in a flash. Your conscience "told" you whether you did what you did with a right or wrong attitude. It all happens in two seconds.

By the way, did you pray for the people at home on your way home from work? Did you ask God to help you as you transition from work life to Home Life? With God's help, a person in a Green job is most apt to have a right attitude at home.

Secondly, another reason a person may only have the potential for a right attitude at home, even if in a Green job, is that pride may have overtaken his or her attitude. Assume he or she is being successful and doing well at work. He or she is beginning to believe he or she is good, and can "conquer the world." Arrogance has slipped into and taken hold of his or her attitude. His or her self-confidence is rising to prideful heights.

As a direct result, he or she has forgotten God . . . forgotten to call on God at work, and on the way home . . . for His Help to serve Him His Way. "God opposes the proud but gives grace to the humble" (1 Peter 5:5). That word "grace" includes His divine assistance.

In a nutshell, such people are too proud to pick up their cross daily, let alone "pick up" the front room, or home play area, or the laundry from the dryer, or rinse and wash dinner dishes. To do so would be too humbling to them.

I have read many writers who have said a person is most susceptible to sin while using their strengths, rather than limitations. This happens because they are not relying on God, but their own personal strength. What a huge lesson for us—using our Greens. We must rely on God both ways (Greens and Reds) and all the time. Satan takes no vacation. The wrong kind of pride is usually arrogance-laced. The right kind of pride is humility-laced.

Other reasons may be advanced for a "right serving attitude" not being automatic for a person now in a Green job. But it is clear that having a right attitude at home, where a person tends to let down, is equally as important as having a right attitude when talking to a neighbor or work associate. But it is always a test, everyday.

While I have no Scripture to prove it, I believe Jesus struggled with this issue at times, although I am sure He dealt with it a lot better than you or I. "He (Jesus) offered up prayers and petitions with loud cries and tears . . . he was heard because of his reverent submission . . . he learned obedience from what he suffered" (Hebrews 5:7-8).

Jesus' reverent submission resulted in His being heard by His Father. Our "reverent submission"—to God, and to individual family members (Ephesians 5:21) will turn potential for a right attitude into reality. While we may not actually experience God in us at that moment, others will see or experience His Divine Nature in us. And that is what counts.

So is having a servant's heart at home one of your Christian Values? If not, should it be?

In a Red Job Now

Early in this chapter we mentioned someone coming home from work either with a Green "tired" or with a Red "tired." And the difference is like day and night. As Fig. 9-a indicates, such a person in Red work has more potential to have a negative attitude than a positive attitude.

This is neither theory nor negative thinking; it is very real. Someone in Red work comes home "dog tired" . . . emotionally, mentally, and even physically drained. As a responsible person, he or she been giving 100% to his or her work, pulling and straining to do a good job while either hating or strongly not liking doing what he or she is.

You see, he or she gets no satisfaction, so no fuel or energy from his or her work. Trying to right a bad attitude, without making the right kind of changes, is hopeless because the problem is the work itself, not the person himself or herself, and his or her attitude. The problem is only solved by changing responsibilities and getting into Green work.

It is a miracle that people in Red jobs do as well as they do at work, with God's help. And most likely they are loaded down with guilt for not having a better attitude, and acting more upbeat. Not to mention feeling guilty about not living up to their own expectations, knowing they should be more positive but are not. So when they cross the threshold into their homes, they are lucky to have enough energy to lift their feet high enough to not trip over the threshold.

Now there are always exceptions, but people in Red jobs will, in all probability, have triple difficulty maintaining a servant's heart at home, not because they are unspiritual, undisciplined, etc., but because their Red job has sapped them of all "umph" and energy.

A servant's heart? Picking up their cross? Why, they can hardly "pick" themselves up off the bed in the morning, let alone pick up their cross when they get home. You may think this is an exaggeration, but it is not. Red work is often the author of negative attitudes and a hopeless spirit. Guilt burdens hearts and slumps shoulders. People in Red jobs have great potential for an ongoing negative attitude.

Someone living with such a person is a true "cross-bearer" or people living with such a person are true "cross-bearers." Living with them is like living next to a volcano—they will erupt at any moment, and often.

It is beyond the scope of this book, but considering only both spouses, think about this. What if both spouses are in Red-for-them jobs? Can you imagine what it is like inside the four walls of their home? No, we can not, unless we have been there ourselves.

Without meaning to sound like a know-it-all, or to diminish God's enabling power, I believe it virtually impossible for someone in Red work to have a servant's heart reasonably consistently. As we have been discussing, it is hard enough for a person in Green work to cultivate such an attitude. I have worked with many people one-on-one who tell me what it is really like in their hearts and homes. It is not a pretty picture.

HOME LIFE . . . <u>RELATIONSHIPS</u>

The focus of this chapter is Home Life. Because Relationships are such a vital subject anywhere and at all times, I am going to talk about Relationships in general for a few paragraphs. Later on in this section, I will apply it to Home Life.

Our Universal Calling includes loving our neighbors. And who is our neighbor? Thinking now for a moment both inside and outside our home, our neighbor is the person next to us now . . . across the dinner table, or riding with us in the car, or sitting next to us in the church pew, or the store clerk, etc.

Love connects; hate disconnects.
Love cares; hate destroys.
Love embraces; hate distances.

When people, with God's sustaining love, reach out to people to care and embrace, they usually form a genuine, positive relationship with someone. It takes two to form a relationship. If a person's initiatives and actions are rebuffed or refused over and over again, no relationship develops. The initiating person still loves him or her, but no relationship forms.

God calls us to even love our enemies and pray for them. Them? Yes, them. Love goes beyond relationships, good or bad. Love goes beyond "like them" or "not like them." God's love in us is the enabling power to carry out God's command to love and pray for our enemies. So we do not pick and choose who to love or when to love. It is God's Universal Principle and Calling at all times.

So, does love always connect? No. Does a genuine, caring, ongoing relationship develop without love? No. But when a person responds, and you continue loving him or her, an emotional connection often forms. You and he or she bond.

Love is foundational to any relationship. A relationship, encircled by love, usually contains (in my opinion) three essentials: respect, trust, and credibility. As you read on, think of the people in your life, including your spouse, parents, children, work associates, etc.

Respect and Trust

Respect means to show regard and consideration for another. Trust means to rely on or have confidence in someone. When God's love trickles into someone's heart and flows outward, it enables him or her to trust people right at the start. Track records are tossed aside.

For example, people should not have to earn one another's trust. That is conditional loving. Instead, one initiates the trust action by being trusting—risking, going out on the limb for another.

Love hears inexperienced people and young children. Love trusts the uneducated and educated. Respect and trust are active. Not to respect and trust disconnects, causing negative relationships to get mired down in the muck of suspicion and hidden agendas. Questions prevail, and action is minimal.

Love that is always calculating discourages people. It disconnects. Relationships suffer. In the comic strip, Tiger says, "That is pretty sneaky," as he sees his opponent Puddinhead beating him playing cards.

"What is pretty sneaky," Puddinhead yells.

Tiger yells back, "You have not cheated once all afternoon." Suspicion arouses suspicion.

To believe people first is to demonstrate trust and respect. It may be very risky and become a source of embarrassment. While Jesus wants us to be secure in Him, he also wants us to move away to where we are exposed and it is treacherous.

"Love one another warmly as Christian brothers, and be eager to show respect for one another" (Romans 12:10). "It [love] always protects, always trusts, always hopes, always perseveres" (I Corinthians 13:7).

Respect and trust, balanced by wisdom and discernment, choose to step out rather than step back and be suspicious. "Love knows no limit to its endurance, no end to its trust" 1 Corinthians 13:7 (Phillips). With God's help, we can trust a lot more than we first thought possible.

Credibility

A brief word about credibility. Credible people are believable. They inspire confidence. Their motives and word meanings don't have to be questioned. Credible people mean what they say and say what they mean.

Their actions speak louder than their words. They follow up. And if they are not, they inform appropriate people rather than leave things hanging or someone else left holding the bag. And if they see they are going to miss a deadline, they tell the affected people beforehand, rather than after the missed deadline. They follow the Golden Rule to a "t."

While an oversimplification, respect, trust, and credibility are among the key essentials of any relationship. Soaked in God's love, they make a person God's instrument, now and everywhere, including home.

Why are positive, loving relationships important?

Positive, caring, loving relationships are important because they are the oil that lubricates working parts—you and me. They reduce friction.

Realistically, relationships have their ups and downs. Where there are people, there will be friction. People rubbing shoulders often rub each other the wrong way. Realistically, relationships are up and down, high and low. Relationships are fragile and imperfect because people are imperfect.

In *No Little People* (Downers Grove, IL: InterVarsity, 1974), Francis Schaeffer wrote: "If we demand, in any of our relationships, either perfection or nothing, we will get nothing."

People living and functioning together disagree. Arguments and disagreements are neither good nor bad unless they continue unsettled. When respect, trust, and credibility are present, patching up differences is a normal happening. Husbands who yell at wives because of a bad day at work sour supper table conversation, but they soon patch up their differ-ences. Wives popping off at husbands who "always" leave the newspaper in the wrong place cause brush fires, but love soon stamps out the flame before it turns into a forest fire.

Differences and disagreements are not disasters. They are the tough grounds that test us. Love is a choice that includes the fostering of genuine relationships. Like many other things, it is no task for the fainthearted or off-and-on-again Christians.

Let's come back Home

Look at fig. 9-a, Carry Over. People in Green work have the most poten-tial for positive relationships. On the other hand, people in Red work have a lot less potential for positive relationships.

If maintaining a servant heart attitude is difficult, then to consistently love others and do things that enhance relationships rather than cause undue friction is an equally, if not greater test. Have you asked yourself if you really love (as God would have you do) your spouse? Your brother? Your teenager? Your nine-year-old?

I know your answer is, "Of course I do. I always have." Really? Have you thought through the implications of what it means to love the right way? Perhaps not. I know I had not until I was confronted. Many years ago I was having a hard time with one of our offspring. All attempts to correct and modify their behavior and my attitude failed. I shared the situation and my frustrations with someone I deeply respected. "What should I do?" I pleaded.

The reply was: "Love them." With lots of confidence I said, "Yes, yes . . . but what should I do?" The answer was the same, "Love them." I began to squirm, unaware the "noose was tightening around my neck." Finally I said: "Perhaps I have not made myself clear. What am I to DO, what action should I take"? You guessed it, the reply was: "Love them."

With the noose around my neck, and without something they (off-spring) were supposed to do, I had to confront myself. I was angry at them . . . and embarrassed about their behavior. But my heart was void of love. I had to do a 180-degree attitude change and begin anew to love them with the right kind of love. I was not loving my neighbor who lived in our home.

Loving people, including family members, is not theory, but action. Whatever we do while loving our neighbor must spring from a heart of love. "... God has poured out his love into our hearts by the Holy Spirit..." (Romans 5:5).

Revisiting fig. 9-a—people in Green work tend to have better people skills, which means better ongoing and positive relationships. On the other hand, people in Red work tend to have not-so-good people relationships.

For all of us, what we say and how we say it has impact on relationships. To help me "guard my words," I often reread Ephesians 4:29: "Do not let any unwholesome talk come out of your mouths, but only what is helpful for building others up according to their needs, that it may benefit those who listen."

People in Red work are often on the emotional edge ... say the wrong thing to them, or they see something going wrong, they "hit the switch" and pop off in an instant. It just happens. The real problem is usually not a spiritual one but a Red job problem.

When I do Red work for extended periods of time, I tend to violate Ephesians 4:29 more often—I get grumpy. I slide into that mode in an unpredictable instant. The words (wrong words) are out of my mouth faster than the blink of an eye.

On the other hand, when I am doing Green work, things "lighten up" for me ... I am less grouchy, more upbeat (not discernible to other people!). I tend to listen more, ask better questions, saying and doing things "according to their needs" (Ephesians 4:29).

The benefits of being in Green work are clear if people value having the potential to be truly loving in their homes, at work, at church, etc. In a nutshell, this is a comparatively doable thing to do for Green people, next to impossible thing to do for Red people.

God does not abandon people in Red jobs. People do not abandon God while in Red jobs. But it sure feels both ways when mired in Red work. Start heading towards your Greens—it will give you hope AND God will help you because He wants you to receive job satisfaction (Ecclesiastes 5:18-20).

HOME LIFE . . . <u>ACTION</u>

We have looked at our Home Life from two dimensions—Attitude and Relationships. Now to the third—Action. Fig. 9-a, Carry-Over indicates people in Green work are more apt to be "helping doers" and self-starters. People in Red work are more apt to be "reluctant doers" and procrastinators.

So a person has to work at work, work at having a serving heart, and work at being loving and fostering positive relationships AND work in the sense of pitching in and getting things done at home. Is this what "WORK-ING out our salvation" is all about? Check out Philippians 2:12. Is not Scripture absolutely profound and practical?

So when a person walks through the door anticipating "doing something," he or she will be faced with either a Green or Red task to do. Said differently, our home "job" requires skills just like our job job. Speaking simplistically, the at-home job is fairly limited in scope, and there are no promotions or raises!

Be that as it may, let us look at one of life's most important job, our At-Home Responsibilities. Look at fig. 9-b. I have divided it into two major areas . . . People-related and Projects/Stuff-related responsibilities. I have matched up Strategy, Tasks, Ideas, and Relationships people with each of these, as you see in fig. 9-b.

But please observe these two words of CAUTION as you review fig. 9-b. The first word of caution is that this is not the best source of information for figuring out whether a Home responsibility is YOUR Green, Yellow, or Red. The best source is your Positive Experiences Listing. And what you do in your home will most likely be different than what I have listed in fig. 9-b, so use what you do in the job match-up process.

The information in fig. 9-b is for people in general, so use this information with eyes wide open. It is not meant to be a standard; instead, meant only to be informative about people in general.

The second word of CAUTION relating to fig. 9-b is that we are looking only at a person's Greens, Yellows, and Reds. It does not take into account a person's Values and Priorities.

So if a responsibility is a Red, a person's Values may click in to help him or her do it and do a better job of it. For example, if caring for children is a Red for a parent, it does not mean he or she always hires someone to do that or automatically delegates it to someone else. He or she does it the best he

AT-HOME RESPONSIBILITES

People-related	Strategy	Tasks	Ideas	Relation-ships
• Building relationships	R	Y or R	Y or R	G
• Taking care of children	R	Y or R	R	G
• Supervising offspring	R	Y	R	G or Y
• Teaching...encouraging	Y	Y	Y or G	G

Projects/Stuff-related	Strategy	Tasks	Ideas	Relation-ships
• Meal/food planning/prep.	R	Y or G	Y or G	Y or R
• Shopping—food, household items, gifts, clothes, etc.	R	Y or G	R	R
• Maintaining/cleaning	R	G	R	R
• Property upkeep—painting, wallpapering, repairing, lawns/gardening, etc.	R	Y or G	Y or R	R
• Schedule keeper, finances administrator	R	Y or G	Y or R	R
• Chauffeuring	R	G	R	Y or G

fig. 9-b

or she can ... first putting on a "servant's apron" (John 13) so he or she will do it with a better attitude. But remember, a Red is a Red. Even though it may be Values-related, a person still will get comparatively little satisfaction from doing it, compared to doing it if it were a Green.

Summarizing fig. 9-b ... At-Home Responsibilities tend not to be a total Green for anyone. But just using this job description, the At-Home Responsibilities seem to match up best for Tasks and Relationships people. For Ideas, it is a weak Yellow. Uh-oh ... and for Strategy people, the match-up is Red.

Recall in Chapter 2 we said there are three benefits of discovering and knowing our Greens, Yellows, and Reds. With such information, a person can:

1. Form realistic expectations,
2. Erase false guilt, and
3. Understand the impact of Greens and Reds on relationships.

Armed with those three benefits, a responsible person is more apt to be a God-pleasing family member contributing to a positive, caring-for-each-other climate in a home.

So know that there are Greens and Reds in the At-Home Responsibilities for everyone. That is a realistic and accurate expectation. Do not feel guilty about a Red. Admit it, and go from there (see Chapter 7). There are things you want to do, there are things you have to do. A Green job will help to make have-to-do tasks a little less difficult.

CHAPTER SUMMARY

A home can be a whirlwind of activity; a home can also be the loneliest place in the world, especially for someone living alone. In either case, having a Green job is a huge asset, a Red job a huge liability.

Our jobs "Carry-Over" into our home life in positive or negative ways. It impacts our attitude, relationships, and actions (or lack thereof). Let us end this chapter by repeating Psalm 101:2 (LB): "I will try to walk a blameless path, but how I need your help, especially in my own home, where I long to act as I should."

CHAPTER 10
APPLICATION: VOLUNTEER LIFE

The *goal* of this chapter is to help you function as a responsible volunteer in light of your Greens, Yellows, and Reds and your present job life and home life commitments.

INTRODUCTION

If you have a full job life (up to 60 hours per week total), and full home life, there is not a lot of time left over for other things like volunteering to serve on your local school committee, or planning board, or in your local church. A recruiter for a volunteer organization said to me: "We get the ragged edge of a person's time."

What he meant was . . . after working all day, and taking care of things at home . . . the time left over is "ragged"—people come to meetings or do things in a tired or hurried manner. Their "best time" went into their jobs and home responsibilities; their "not-so-good time" was given to volunteer work.

Assuming there is some truth to this person's statement, and even if you disagree with it, the fact remains there usually is not a lot of time left over for volunteer work. And yet, most responsible people feel they should make some contribution, along with others, to a worthy cause, or a people-helping agency, or to the local church, and the like.

Believers in Christ believe everyone should be supportively involved in the local church, the least being attending a weekly worship service . . . but more, taking on jobs and tasks as volunteers. While so doing, they may serve in some official or appointed manner, e.g. serving on a committee or board, or chairing a board, or taking care of finances, etc. Or they may serve in unofficial ways such as welcoming visitors or new worshipers, or stepping in to sub when someone is ill, or willingly setting up or taking down chairs and tables, driving people to and from, praying for people, and the like.

Additionally, a believer in Christ often feels he should serve in his community or local school system, for instance. The picture is getting messy, a lifestyle "on the edge." And to top it all off, a person can feel guilty for overworking as a volunteer, and overlooking important commitments at home, with relatives, etc.

Now toss into the mix people having to take care of elderly parents, or relatives, or a neighbor, or parents have physically, emotionally, or mentally challenged children, and life tends to get complex, very complex. Their time is schedule-driven. Time to be alone with God in Bible study/prayer/meditation is at a premium. Oh yes, one more thing! Your physical conditioning program . . . there goes several more hours each week.

So right at the outset, let us admit we have a potential time problem in the making, and ironically enough, the more responsible a person, the greater his or her potential to become over-committed as a volunteer. And what suffers? Our home life and our spiritual life. I once heard this saying: "Isn't it interesting how people can trip over people at home rushing out to serve others!" The point is: it is often more appealing for someone to do volunteer work, along with the publicity and attention that often gets, rather than stay at home and helping and serving needy people there. Did I hear you say being a quiet missionary for Jesus in our own homes may be our most testing and demanding responsibility?

AVOID OVEREXTENDING WITH "1 PLUS ONE"

Rather than ignore how responsible people may over-commit and get head over heels in volunteer work, let us confront the issue now so that we will not discourage, but rather encourage, those who should be volunteering and also help them keep their job life and home life in their rightful priority.

In Chapter 7, we said someone was overextending when he or she worked 60 or so hours weekly, including commute time. This being the case, most likely some of his or her personal values and priorities were going unrealized; that includes having little time to volunteer.

However, people can also overextend in their volunteer lives. Paul's work week totaled 55 hours on average. He came to me concerned about his total life—job life, home life, and volunteer life. He used words like stretched, frazzled, no time to myself, and the like. Familiar words?

He told me he had five—yes, five—things he was doing as a volunteer; all five were time- consuming jobs. In other words, it was not just a committee meeting once a month and then go home. Each job consumed from four to ten hours monthly. Paul was overextended because of the amount of time spent volunteering each month.

I pointed out to Paul a concept I learned and interpreted from a book *The Decision Makers* (Nashville, Abington, 1974) by Lyle Schaller. His point was a person cannot be effective having several volunteer jobs at one time while having a full-time job.

Paul said this about his five volunteer jobs: "I feel as though I am not accomplishing anything in any of them." Yes, his wheels were spinning. He felt out of control.

After reading Schaller's book, and to help people like Paul, you, and me, I have come up with the "J plus one" concept. The letter "J" means Job. One means one time-consuming volunteer job. The "J plus one" concept means a person can do only one time-consuming (involving time and follow-up, in addition to the usual committee meetings) volunteer responsibility effectively, in addition to full-time job (J) responsibilities.

I was at "J plus three" for several years. I never felt at peace about it. I did not feel I was doing a good job at two of them. I felt pressured and frustrated.

While I realize people spend varying amounts of time on the job, the right "formula" for you might be different . . . say, J plus two. All I am trying to point out is be aware of the impact too many volunteer jobs might have on your other life's priorities.

Few people will help you apply the J plus one concept. Most people only help you overextend. I hate the saying: "To get something done, ask a busy person." Do we ever wonder how what we are asking them to do might impact their personal values and priorities, relationships, walk with God, etc.?

Returning to Paul—over the next year he reduced his volunteer work from five jobs to two. He said: "It is the difference between night and day. I am back." What he meant was he was back spending quality time with people, spending more time in personal Bible study and prayer, and feeling less tension with people at work.

So amid the realities of life's often demanding commitments and schedules, keep in mind the J plus One Concept so you can maintain some semblance of balance in your life. Let us return now to the main subject at hand, volunteering.

WHAT IS A VOLUNTEER?

Let's first define volunteer (from the dictionary). The word "volunteer" means: a person who 1. offers himself for a service without obligation to do so (offers of his own free will) and 2. performs a service willingly and without pay. In a nutshell, volunteering is an act of helping, not getting, although we often "get" more in intrinsic rewards than we "give out."

Volunteers volunteer. They are neither heavy-handedly persuaded or given inducements to help. They may have been recruited or encouraged in terms of being made aware of a need, but a volunteer steps out and volunteers, saying in effect: "I want to do that."

They should serve willingly, from the heart, rather than doing something because they feel guilty, or because they have some hidden agenda, like looking for sales prospects, or another job, or volunteering to prove someone either wrong or right. Volunteer's motives are literally pure . . . to serve, period.

Opportunities for service as a volunteer abound . . . community organizations, non-profit agencies, hospitals, para-church organizations, churches, and the list goes on. As in our Job Life and Home Life, our calling as volunteers to any of these is to please God and glorify Him . . . nothing more, nothing less. Because this is such a broad subject and to keep us focused, let us center our discussion in this chapter around being a volunteer in a local church. Many of the things we will bring out should apply in other volunteer settings.

CLARIFY YOUR REASONS FOR VOLUNTEERING

Thinking now about a church setting, as believers we have a number of reasons for volunteering, but in my view, two reasons rise to the forefront. One, we volunteer out of deep, deep *gratitude* to God for sending His Son and changing our hearts and lives. "God so loved the world . . ." (John 3:16a). Contemplate what He did for you during one of your alone times with God. Meditate on it. When I do, all I can say is "Thank you Lord." "Give thanks . . . for this is God's will . . ." (1 Thessalonians 5:18).

A grateful, thankful heart pleases God. So I volunteer because I am so grateful to God for His love and goodness. I see volunteering as an opportunity, not an obligation. And it took me years to make that distinction. But what a world of difference it makes in my attitude viewing volunteer work as opportunity, rather than "just another job to do" or something I am "supposed" to do or a way to simply "carry my weight" or a share of the load.

Two, the second reason for volunteering is similar to reason one . . . I volunteer because I am *devoted* to God. "Serve the Lord with a heart full of devotion." Romans 12:11b (TEV). My devotion centers on and around God. My passion is God, period. I am to love Him devotedly, from the heart. That devotion draws me to Him or inspires me to desire to serve Him, not only as a volunteer (this chapter's focus), but also in other settings, e.g. at work or home.

Our Universal Calling includes loving God (Matthew 22:37), devotedly and passionately. Then look at what He will do: "God has poured out his love into our hearts by the Holy Spirit . . ." (Romans 5:5). My human love is limited; God's love, that He "pours into our hearts by the Holy Spirit" is limitless. That limitless concept causes us to be overcome with gratitude, prompting us to volunteer—raise our hands, to say: "Here I am, Lord, send me." In so doing, we love our neighbors (Universal Calling—Matthew 22:39) with His love enabling us to do things or reach out and care way beyond our initial expectations.

In turn, we become "foot-washers" (John 13:14), not "foot-draggers." We serve humbly, not arrogantly. Our attitude is one of gratitude, not "pride" because "they" asked me to do it. We do it not to prove anything to ourselves or to others. We serve because we know we are unworthy of His grace, not because we are needed so desperately to fill a slot or position.

THE CARRY-OVER PRINCIPLE APPLIES HERE TOO

As you might expect, the Carry-over Principle applies not only to Home Life, but also to our Volunteer Life (fig. 9-a, Chapter 9). Recall we said a person's job and level of job satisfaction (or lack thereof) carries over into and affects off-the-job life, including his or her Home Life (last chapter) and his or her willingness to be a faithful volunteer.

So a person in a Green job comes home with a "Green tired"—tired but still upbeat and positive.

A person in a Red job comes home with a "Red tired"—tired, exhausted, and often discouraged.

So generally speaking, a person in Green work would tend to be most open and willing to do volunteer work (within reason, of course). A person in Red work would tend to be less open and willing to do volunteer work.

Of course, just because someone is in Green work now does not mean he or she will accept what a volunteer recruiter may be asking him or her to do. And just because someone is in Red work now does not mean he or she will not accept what a volunteer recruiter may be asking him or her to do. All I am pointing out is that a person's level of job satisfaction (high or low) may influence someone's willingness to consider doing something in the first place.

The many people I have worked with over the years in Red jobs at work and doing time-consuming volunteer jobs feel "run over" by life. So we need to be careful about what we expect from ourselves and other people now in Red work.

So I repeat. Being in Green work is so essential. Not only then do we have more potential for a close walk with God, but we also have more potential to be willing and cooperative volunteers helping and reaching out to people. Does this please God? Will God be glorified? Yes.

OUR GREENS AND REDS AND SPIRITUAL GIFTS

What to do specifically in the church as a volunteer inevitably brings up the subject of spiritual gifts. Over the years I have studied this area comprehensively, and talked to lots of knowledgeable people about it. As a result, I have settled into a belief system about them which has helped me focus on "asking for the Holy Spirit" (Luke 11:13 . . . sound familiar?), rather than wondering what spiritual gift I may be using or what others tell me I am using. More about this later.

In the next few pages, I will be explaining what I believe about spiritual gifts and their relationship to Greens and Reds. Please keep an open mind as you read this; if you decide to "dump" what I am saying because you hold to a different view, fine. In my view, it will not change one iota your Individual Calling.

As background, we need to remember that Paul (in 1 Corinthians) brought up this subject of spiritual gifts because of the "abuse" of spiritual gifts by the people who were causing division and conflict in the church. They got bogged down in details—spiritual gifts. Their focus was inward, on themselves, rather than upward, on God. What they were doing was not God-pleasing.

SPIRITUAL GIFTS

So what are spiritual gifts? They are special abilities given to believers by the Holy Spirit to build up the church, the Body of Christ. "Try to excel in gifts [spiritual gifts] that build up the church . . ." (1 Corinthians 14:12b). And as we will be saying in a moment, spiritual gifts are given by the Holy Spirit, so it follows that non-believers do not have these special abilities, because they do not have the Holy Spirit.

Read these next two verses closely. "Now to each one the manifestation of the Spirit is given for the common good" (1 Corinthians 12:7). Verse two: "All these [spiritual gifts] are the work of one and the same Spirit, and he gives them to each man, just as he determines." (I Corinthians 12:11).

Lets' summarize the last two paragraphs with these two conclusions:

1. Spiritual gifts are meant to benefit the BODY OF CHRIST; they are meant for the common good (I Corinthians 12:7). The other side is: spiritual gifts are not meant to enhance one's influence among believers or even to make people feel good. Spiritual gifts benefit others, not themselves. They are "others directed," not "me-directed."

2. Spiritual gifts are given to each believer as DETERMINED BY THE HOLY SPIRIT. Did you get that? God, through the Holy Spirit, is the Master Distributor of spiritual gifts. He does it just as "He determines" (1 Corinthians 12:11). This means you and I have absolutely no say in it. God decides; God determines.

In a nutshell, not only is God sovereignly ruling all things, big and small, but He is also in charge of the world of spiritual gifts. He (not we) determines their distribution. Let us quickly and briefly switch gears and discuss a person's natural talents.

NATURAL TALENTS

We touched on this area of natural talents in Chapter 2, but I want to bring it up here in a different context. Natural talents (or natural gifts) are a person's natural abilities. A person's Greens are their natural talents.

The word "natural" carries with it the idea of occurring in conformity with the ordinary course of nature . . . normal or usual. It is "normal" for people to have natural talents. They equip people to do some things well (their niche) and so contribute to people's well-being and society in general.

Natural talents are innate to each person. Natural talents are discoverable. Because they operate in the natural world, we can use natural means (logic) to discover them, as we did while identifying Greens. All people, believers and non-believers, have natural talents—Greens. This is the way God made all of us.

SPIRITUAL AND NATURAL REALMS

Non-believers operate in the natural realm, because until they commit their lives to Christ, they do not have the Holy Spirit. On the other hand, believers, with the help of the Holy Spirit, operate in the spiritual realm. Have you ever wondered why spiritual gifts are called *spiritual* gifts? One reason may be as a reminder to treat them in a spiritual manner, not "natural" manner, e.g. logic, etc. The Holy Spirit cannot be put into a logic box; the Holy Spirit has a will of His own ("just as He determines"—1 Corinthians 12:11).

We treat them in a spiritual manner when we use "tools" like faith, trust, confession, love, and the like. In the context of this discussion, we treat spiritual gifts in a spiritual manner when we trust or totally depend on the Holy Spirit to do "just as He determines," in terms of spiritual gift distribution to believers.

In my view, we do not discover spiritual gifts; we do not use logic or checklists to pinpoint a person's spiritual gifts from three or four incomplete listings in the Bible. To do so is to make "natural" what is spiritual. To do so is to put God in a box and so run the risk of limiting the operation of His Holy Spirit in our lives.

In a nutshell, I believe we should stop trying to discover our spiritual gifts; their distribution is God's territory, not yours or mine. Our focus needs to be on being Christian, reverencing God in our hearts, evidencing the Fruit of the Spirit (Galatians 5:22-23) day-in, day-out, and knowing and using our Greens and some of our Reds. In turn, our focus will be on being active, consistent contributors (volunteers) in His church.

SPIRITUAL GIFTS DO NOT REPLACE NATURAL TALENTS (GREENS)

When a person receives Christ, he or she also receives the Holy Spirit so is a candidate for spiritual gifts. When a person becomes a believer, he or she does not run to the nearest mountain top and fling his or her natural talents (Greens) into the wind before responsibly functioning as a volunteer in a church. His or her natural talents remain intact; they do not change. What does change when someone receives Christ are such things as attitude, motives, life purpose, interests, goals, lifestyle, etc.

So when a person walks into church to worship, or attends a committee meeting, or sings in the choir, or cleans up after a church fellowship dinner, he or she does not leave his or her Greens and Reds at the church doorstep and pick them up on the way out. No, each person brings who he or she is, his or her natural talents and limitations, with them into Church AND wherever he or she is serving Christ.

Please read closely. At any moment, God may choose to distribute a spiritual gifts(s) through me. In that sense, I am His instrument there; the vehicle He uses will be through my Greens and Reds. See fig. 10-a.

fig. 10-a

A key conclusion . . .

NATURAL TALENTS (GREENS) AND NATURAL LIMITATIONS (REDS) ARE THE VEHICLE FOR SPIRITUAL GIFTS

Looked at one way, natural talents/natural limitations and spiritual gifts are worlds apart. One is discoverable, the other is not. One is present in us all the time; the other's presence in us is unknowable—their presence or absence in us is a function of the Holy Spirit.

Looked at another way, natural talents/natural limitations and spiritual gifts work like hand and glove. The hand—always with us (natural talents/ natural limitations) is the vehicle for the glove (spiritual gifts). Gloves are not worn by people all the time. And whether or not you believe you need or even have "gloves" may be a function of your spiritual gift theology!

Let's switch gears a bit. As we think about believers having Greens and Reds, which are vehicles or the means used by the Holy Spirit to distribute spiritual gifts, I would like to suggest that it is absolutely essential not to lose sight of two things: (1) what it means to be spiritual people, and (2) what spiritual service means.

Briefly stated, *spiritual people* are those who acknowledge (a.) their need for God (Matthew 6:33), and (b.) dependency on God (Hebrews 11:6), and also (c.) strongly desire a close and growing relationship with God (Colossians 2:6). What they value most is their walk with God; they trust God (John 14:1) and His Holy Spirit.

Briefly stated, *spiritual service* is work done for God by spiritual people using spiritual means to accomplish spiritual ends. They view spiritual service as a privilege, rather than a burdensome job.

THE GREEN LIGHT CONCEPT AND SPIRITUAL SERVICE

So within the framework of this discussion, we can conclude there are two kinds of spiritual service—work done for God by spiritual people. One is Green spiritual service, the other Red spiritual service. Green spiritual service uses a person's Greens. So if visiting people is your Green (it is a Red for a lot of us!), then while visiting newcomers, you would be involved in Green spiritual service.

Red spiritual service uses a person's Reds. One of my Reds is "greeting people" or doing anything PR related. So when I usher, I am involved in Red spiritual service. Recall we said a person's Individual Calling includes using our Greens <u>and</u> some of our Reds.

Both Green and Red spiritual service are energized by the same SOURCE—the Holy Spirit. This is a key concept. Do not overlook what that should mean to us as we are directly involved in Green and Red spiritual service. As Paul wrote (2 Corinthians 3:5): "Our competence comes from God."

Here is a diagram to express this SAME SOURCE concept (fig. 10-b).

Here is an example. Suppose Ellen's Greens include writing and illustrating, and Reds include teaching and visiting. In her church right now there are no job opportunities that will use her Greens.

There is, however, a need for fifth-grade Sunday School teachers; she accepts the teaching responsibility. When a spiritual person engages in Red spiritual service, she will be energized and enabled by the Holy Spirit. She may not teach at A level, but with the Lord's help, she can be His person and instrument with each class member. With extra preparation, most apt to teach at B level, rather than C level (normal for people doing Red work). And as a spiritual person, she prays faithfully for each student, as well as family members.

By knowing Greens and Reds, a person can form realistic expectations about both his or her feelings toward a responsibility and how well he or she will tend to do it. We need to be ready. Spiritual people doing spiritual service are most apt to be "doers." Note 2 Timothy 2:21: "If a man cleanses himself from the latter [ignoble purposes, previous verse], he will be an instrument for noble purposes, made holy, useful to the Master and prepared to do any good work." The good work may be Green or Red work.

As you have already gathered by now, I do not know what my spiritual gifts are. Getting rid of the notion that I have to discover them has been so freeing for me. I never did feel right about saying: "These are my spiritual gifts." I always asked myself: "Who am I to think I know them"? I have no difficulty telling someone my Greens and Reds, but spiritual gifts are an entirely different, yes sacred, matter.

SAME SOURCE CONCEPT

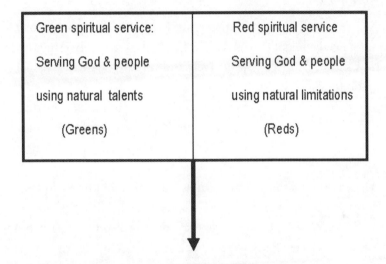

fig. 10-b

I know many people believe differently; I respect their beliefs about this subject. But I am of the school that I am an instrument or vehicle of the Holy Spirit, and that is good enough for me.

Three illustrations of spiritual people involved in Green and Red spiritual service

Here are three illustrations of three different volunteers who are spiritual people directly involved in Green and Red spiritual service.

Illustration one

Suppose Janet is suddenly inspired (Holy Spirit operating!) to cook a meal for a needy neighbor. Cooking is her Red. While delivering the meal on a tray, she feels moved to sensitively and verbally share the Gospel with the person to whom she is ministering.

Here is a person involved in Red spiritual service; under the direction of the Holy Spirit, she "evangelizes," perhaps for the first time in a long time. This caring, cooking neighbor has been praying for this neighbor for over two years.

Does it really matter that she know her spiritual gift to do this? No. Does it really matter that she did not wonder afterwards what spiritual gift she used? No. What does matter is that she was a spiritual person doing spiritual service. Her Reds were a vehicle of the Holy Spirit, perhaps to bring into operation some spiritual gift. She was about the work of "making disciples" and pleasing God.

Illustration two

Chuck, a seventeen-year-old, purchased his first car . . . a six-year-old "bucket of bolts." Thirty days later the car develops engine problems. A deacon, Mr. Smith, who knows cars (his Green is fixing mechanical things) stops by one Saturday to help repair the engine.

A good conversation develops between them. Soon the teenager is telling about a personal problem he is facing. The deacon, under the direction of the Holy Spirit, sensitively passes along some wisdom (spiritual gift?) that seems to hit the nail on the head—just what the teenager seemed to need to hear. By the way, they did get the clunker going again.

Was the deacon encouraging (spiritual gift)? Perhaps. Helping (spiritual gift)? Yes. Teaching (spiritual gift)? Perhaps. Being discerning, and exercising the spiritual gift of wisdom? Perhaps. But again, the significant dimension is he was being a spiritual person doing spiritual service, whether or not some spiritual gift was in operation.

By faith we believe, however, that the Holy Spirit was present in the deacon as he worked and spoke. His natural talents—Greens were a vehicle for spiritual gifts, if in fact any spiritual gift was in operation. In my view, we should not get all tangled up trying to decide what spiritual gifts a person may have used at X moment in time. Let's keep our focus upward, on God, who is the Source of all good that is done.

Illustration three

Singing solos is Kim's Green. She usually performs before audiences of 200 people; as she sings, people are usually moved and blessed. Is perhaps the spiritual gift of exhortation or encouragement accompanying her singing?

Here is a person using her natural talent (Green) as a vehicle for one or several spiritual gifts that may come into operation by the Holy Spirit. She is a spiritual person. While we may not know if a spiritual gift accompanied her singing, we do know she sang with help from the Holy Spirit. Her heart is soft, open to His Work in her life. And it may not surprise you that she has a team of people praying for her, both beforehand and while she is performing.

Singing solos is also Dale's Green. He sings before audiences like Kim's. Everyone agrees Dale is a better performer than Kim. After Dale performs, there is usually "polite applause." As they say: "It was wonderful but . . . ." The audience is usually impressed, but something is missing. What is lacking is a spiritual person; in all probability, no spiritual gifts accompanied his use of his natural talents.

A mini-summary. I believe God wants spiritual people to responsibly use their Greens and some of their Reds in spiritual service. They serve because they want to, not because they must. God's love in them inspires and excites them. God not only loves a cheerful giver (!), but also a cheerful server. So focus your attention on God Almighty and His Holy Spirit, rather than whether or not a particular spiritual gift is being used.

FEWER CHURCH JOB OPPORTUNITIES

Out there in the wide world, there tends to be a wide variety of options for someone in full-time work. In other words, hundreds of jobs are "out there." There may be numerous options that would utilize a person's Greens and enable him or her to realize his or her Individual Calling.

However, in the local church, there are fewer volunteer job options, compared to the more numerous full-time opportunities. This often means there are fewer Green volunteer opportunities and a lot more Red volunteer opportunities.

Illustrating this a bit, would a local church need for several hours weekly a mechanical engineer, product designer, computer programmer, building contractor, police officer, lawyer, dentist, auditor, system analyst, statistician, fashion designer, tool maker, etc., etc.? Most likely the answer is, "Not very often."

However, there is a big difference between spending 40 to 60 hours weekly in a full-time job, and spending six or seven hours weekly in a volunteer job. Sticking with the idea that most volunteer church jobs are Red, there is a world of difference between a Red full-time job and a Red volunteer job in that less time is spent volunteering than at full-time work.

This "time-doing-it" notion does not change anything in terms of a volunteer job being Red or Green. But it follows that it would be somewhat less difficult long-term doing a weekly short stint of Red work as a volunteer than a full week of Red work.

So how about you? Would most church volunteer jobs be Red, or would some be Green? To find out, let's call on our old friend, your Positive Experiences Listing. Did you list a church job there as a Positive Experience? If so, most likely that kind of job is at least a Yellow, perhaps a Green.

On the other hand, suppose you did not list a church experience as a Positive Experience. Does this mean all church jobs are Red. No, no. For example, I listed several teaching experiences as Positive Experiences. They were all in a business setting. However, teaching remains a Green, whether in a business or church setting (within reason, of course).

So look at them, and see if there are things you did there that are transferable to a volunteer setting . . . in this case, the local church. In the long run, you will tend to be more effective doing something Green or Green-related, rather than doing just Reds.

So this brings us to two realities. One, there is always work to be done in the local church by willing volunteers. Two, in the process of doing that work, we could be involved in either Green or Red Spiritual Service. As just pointed out, we can expect a sizable hunk of what we do to be Red work. This leads us to the important question: What should an individual do specifically in the local church as a volunteer?

DECIDING WHAT TO DO AS A CHURCH VOLUNTEER

In my view, there are no pat answers to the issue of what a person should do specifically in his local church. In the decision process, we should, at a minimum, keep the following in mind:

Do I have the *time*? How much time weekly will it take? How does the "J plus One" Concept apply?

Check your *motives*. Are you serving out of deep gratitude for what God and Christ have done for you? Is your motive to just serve because it is an opportunity, and not just a job to do?

In the decision process, also consider the following:

1. Do not make a quick yes/no decision. **Think and pray** about it for at least a week.
2. Ask yourself: What is it that I really **desire doing for the Lord** in our church?
3. Are the responsibilities you are considering **Green or Red?** Review again your Positive Experiences Listing.
4. If applicable, find out the two or three **job priorities** in order to form realistic expectations of what is required and expected of you?
5. Is this something that really **interests** me? If no, and I accept doing it, do I understand my desire to continue doing it may drop off, which should cause me to seek God's help in this matter, especially during "drop-off" times?

While making a decision, also consider the following: Avoid *Green Overdose*. While it may seem unrealistic, a person may be doing mainly Greens on-the-job. By Friday night, he or she needs a break from his or her Greens, and just do something else—yes, even Reds!

So if a person takes another Green job as a volunteer, he or she may suffer from Green Overdose—just too much of a good thing. So a person may volunteer to do something in the church, just to do something different from what he or she does during the week.

Here is an example. If someone is a nurse (Green) all week long, then to volunteer in the church to mainly be "Care Outreach Nurse" five hours weekly may be the straw that breaks the camel's back. Instead, he or she may want to do something totally different (within reason, of course).

Here is another example. If someone is a elementary school teacher during the week (assuming that is his or her Green), the last thing he or she may want to do is teach kids Sunday morning. Instead, he or she may want to volunteer to do something totally different (again, within reason).

On the other hand, if someone is in a Red job during the week, as mentioned in Chapter 8, it is a virtual must that he or she do something Green-realizing as a volunteer (someplace) . . . just to get a little hope and Green into his or her life. More Red as a volunteer would tend to make an already miserable life even more miserable, if that were possible.

Repeating what we said earlier in this chapter: people do not shed their natural talents—Greens, Yellows, and Reds—and suddenly and mysteriously become clothed in spiritual gifts just by crossing the threshold of a church or while visiting a needy neighbor, or sticking their heads under the hood of a car to help someone. Instead, people bring who they are—Greens, Yellows, and Reds into every dimension of spiritual service, whether singing in the choir, counting money, or recruiting volunteers.

OUR NON-FRIEND SATAN

This could have been included at any point in this book, but I will include it now because I think Satan will do anything and everything to discourage us from functioning as responsible, willing-to-serve volunteers.

So while deciding whether or not to do something, he may whisper things like: "Don't do it, it is your Red . . . you really don't have the time . . . others could do it so much better . . . let someone else do it . . . you have done enough already . . ." etc., etc.

While undertaking a responsibility, he may whisper things like: "Don't do it now, rest . . . don't go visit them or call them, it may interrupt something important they are doing . . . you are too tired to pray now," etc., etc.

From time to time, I like visiting people in their homes, usually early evening. Don't think that Satan goes to bed after I have had supper. Instead, he is lurking right by my church directory as I review names to visit . . . telling me, "It is too cold to visit, or too hot, or that I might bother them tonight, or I am too tired," and a hundred other things that may come to mind. I believe Satan the slanderer tries every tactic to stall us. "Resist him (Satan), standing firm in the faith . . ." (1 Peter 5:9). By acting in faith and getting into the car and going out, I am "standing firm in the faith."

If I sit down in an easy chair after supper, even for a few minutes, with the intention of going in five minutes, Satan has won. I seldom move again that evening!

SUCCESS

"How successful have I been as a volunteer?" you may ask. I don't know and I never ask. I believe that is God's territory, not mine. Let His Spirit do His work. I hope I am an instrument of His while doing Red Spiritual Service, and from time to time, Green Spiritual Service. Doing it in His Name, and being a responsible, credible worker in the process is my goal.

A FINAL THOUGHT

Changing the subject a bit. Think of all the dear servers who, week-in, week-out, take care of aging parents, or a needy neighbor, or children or a spouse who need extra time, care, and attention. Such people are at "J plus two" (at least) without an official church "job."

A person should not feel guilty because he or she does not have an official, designated church job. Not only is there a huge need for dear servers to take care of needy people, but such people can literally DO many important unofficial jobs like making a periodic visit to or phoning someone, or thanking people for helping/serving (e.g. choir members), writing a note of appreciation, encouraging people . . . just to name a few things.

Spiritual people who love God innately desire to be involved in Spiritual Service. They spot opportunities, and quietly do their thing—be it Green or Red. They do not first ask: "Will this use my spiritual gift?" They consistently seek God's help, whether doing big or little things, noticed or unnoticed things. The Holy Spirit is their enabler while they use their Greens and Reds. God bless willing volunteers whose first and only passion is God himself!

CHAPTER SUMMARY

Volunteers do work that is official—like secretary, vice chairperson, trustee, etc., but they also do lots of work in an unofficial capacity—driving someone there, calling someone, baking, fixing, visiting, encouraging, writing notes . . . to name just a few things.

But all volunteers have at least two things in common. One, they serve God and people from a God-loving heart, and with a love-from-God heart. Two, they use their Greens and Reds while actively serving. Their main desire is to be "carriers of the Holy Spirit," not "carriers of some special gift." And while serving, they usually get to know people, and others get to know them. A special bond develops. Teamwork happens, not by plan, but because responsible people are "busy" being spiritual people doing spiritual service.

CHAPTER 11
APPLICATION: STUDENT JOB LIFE

The *goal* of this brief chapter is to help a student either clarify or narrow down what to major in at school—be it college, or grad school, or medical school, etc. A *secondary goal* is the hope this information can also be helpful to those who may be "scraping by" in school, and wondering why they are not "grasping things" like they should. In either case, as you read this, we must take as a given that a student is relatively mature and responsible for his or her age and life circumstances.

INTRODUCTION

Our Individual Calling includes using our Greens and some of our Reds "all the time"—on the job, at home, and while volunteering. Now we turn to another type of full-time job, that of student.

When developing Values-Priorities as part of their Individual Calling, many people list as one of their values "growing and developing" or "continue learning and improving." We should all be life-long students. We are usually full-time students through high school, college, grad school, etc., then part-time students thereafter.

This book is designed for people struggling in their jobs. But many people not only struggle in their jobs, but also struggle in their student jobs (like yours truly did) as well. So a high school senior or college sophomore, in a "struggle" mode, will feel "everyone" knows exactly what they will do after graduation, what they will major in, etc.; at least it seems that way.

Perhaps you have a son or daughter struggling in school. They are scraping by with C's, an occasional B, and a D sprinkled in here and there. Their hard work and discipline is not paying off in terms of good grades. They feel guilty for letting you down; they feel guilty for letting themselves down.

People who feel guilty often withdraw or seek peer approval, at times from people who may be poor influences on them, especially during formative years. So we are dealing with serious issues.

Let's tackle this struggling student issue by using tools we are familiar with—first by doing a Job Match-up, in this case the job of student, and then giving you helps via Job Decision Checklist for full-time students.

STUDENT JOB MATCH-UP

As a person walks into the classroom or study room, he or she again does not drop off his or her Greens and Reds at the door, and suddenly become clothed in "student gifts" (just a term I made up for this discussion) like researching, writing, problem solving, and the like. Instead, as before, we bring who we are in terms of Greens and Reds into the classroom with us.

So if a person is Relationships, with Skills that include building relationships and visiting, this fact remains as he or she sits, listens, takes notes (a few at least) during a class lecture. But notice that person between classes. He or she "pops up" out of his or her seat and starts visiting with classmates. He or she comes to life using his or her Greens. He or she slumps in his or her seat taking notes, pondering "heavy stuff," and the like.

But look over there! Several students still have their noses in a book . . . ingesting information and soaking it in. They are savoring every minute of the lecture and between classes studying the book. Such people tend to be Ideas people, assuming their Greens include researching, studying, thinking reflectively, and the like.

The point is obvious. Here too in the classroom, a person is usually drawn, like paper clips to a magnet, to do things that give him or her satisfaction. Relationships people are usually drawn to people, rather than primarily to studying and researching. On the other hand, Ideas people tend to be drawn to ideas and information, rather than primarily to interacting with people.

STUDENT JOB MATCH-UP

Responsibility	Strategy	Tasks	Ideas	Relationships
• Studying	R	Y	G	R
• Writing term papers	R	Y or R	G	R
• Best at cramming for tests	G	R	Y or R	R
• Taking tests	G	R	Y or G	R
• Good study habits	R	G	G	R
• Being in/attending class	R	Y or G	G	R
• Visiting between classes	R	R	Y or R	G
• Having roommates	Y	R	Y	G

OVERALL MATCH-UP

fig. 11-a

Look at fig. 11-a, Student Job Match-up. This lists the typical responsibilities of a student and how well that responsibility matches up with S, T, I, and R's Greens. I want to emphasize STRONGLY that this information is very general, and there are many exceptions. But over the long haul, these are at least some of the main tendencies of people in their jobs as students.

We of course know that there are many influences on how well a student applies himself or herself during school or college. They include his or her level of maturity, how well he or she can discipline himself or herself, his or her sense of responsibility, the level of difficulty of the subject at hand, and the like. While often overlooked, another significant influence on student performance is what we bring to the classroom—Greens and Reds.

Summarizing briefly, people usually do not automatically "take to the books" because the student job may use more of their Reds than Greens. So looking just through the eyes of the Green Light Concept, Ideas people tend to do well in school because the job of student matches up well with their Greens—satisfaction and skills. And here we must assume their major is something that interests them.

For the rest of us, the job of student tends to be Yellow or Red. Recall what we said about Dealing with Reds in Chapter 7, especially Guidelines like "Planning Plus" and "Holding Ourselves Accountable." To keep up with the "curve raisers," many of us have to study a lot longer (than someone in his or her Green) and exercise "beaucoup" discipline to keep up with our studies and assignments, and in so doing, getting decent grades (at least B).

To help us deal with our Reds and realize our learning goals, I have put together a summary of "How People Learn," (fig. 11-b). These are general tendencies, but developed in hopes of giving people insight into how they will learn most effectively in light of their Greens and Reds.

HOW PEOPLE LEARN

	STRATEGY	TASKS	IDEAS	RELATION-SHIPS
Tend to **LEARN** best while...	•Scanning, highlighting	•Reading practical principles, proven-in-practice methods	•Studying, in-depth research via books, experimentation, sightings	•Sharing/ exchanging ideas one-on-one
	•Reading summarized overviews	•Referring to how-to instructions, becoming proficient at doing them "by the book"	•Reflecting on, conceptualizing	•Seminars with lots of small group interaction
	•Reading industry magazines, newsletters		•Interacting in-depth one-on-one	•Reading people-related books, magazines
	•Attending short, e.g. two-hour seminars	•Using self-instructional texts	•Attending seminars covering a subject comprehensively	•Observing people's attitudes/ behavior, lifestyle

fig. 11-b

HOW PEOPLE LEARN

	STRATEGY	TASKS	IDEAS	RELATION-SHIPS
TIDBITS: will tend to...	•Learn between times rather than in a planned, scheduled manner •Avoid details, how-to's	•Want to know all the details •Avoid advanced, complex subjects •Study at own pace, or independently	•Feast on complex subjects, hate simple subjects •Want to know it broadly and in-depth	•Avoid highly technical or complex subjects •Avoid self-study programs
LIBRARIES will tend to...	•Avoid libraries...if goes and stays too long, will have difficulty sitting still	•Go to how-to section and read by themselves	•"Live" in library; savor entire experience	•Read about people-related issues; if stays too long may start talking to people! Shhh!

fig. 11-b(2)

PICKING AN EDUCATIONAL MAJOR

For some people, deciding what to major in is ducks soup, as in "I have always known this is what I want to do." For many of us, picking an educational major is an ongoing battle, often switching from one semester to the next. Plus there are expectations put on students by teachers, parents, friends, etc. that often puts stress and pressure on someone.

Last month, Steve, a high school senior asked me to help him select a college major. He completed his Positive Experiences Listing, coming up with Tasks as his Greens, and Ideas his Red. His parents are both medical doctors and have hinted it would be nice if their offspring followed in their footsteps. This responsible Tasks person feels "under the gun."

You see, his Positive Experiences are loaded with mechanical stuff—fixing, modifying and "souping up" cars. Nothing in him is medically related. His main interest is cars, based on the facts of his Positive Experiences. His college major should be in the mechanical/technical field, with perhaps a business minor. He loves doing hands-on mechanical work—yes, getting his hands dirty. A technical college or school would also be a good choice for him.

His parents, while at first disappointed, now see the right direction for their offspring . . . and are busy visiting appropriate technical colleges and schools. While studying is his Red, we should expect him to at least get solid C's in college, perhaps B's. But the negative pressure of studying in a field he has no interest in—medical—is off his shoulders. The parents are acting maturely also.

So to pick a major, people follow the same process we used choosing a job . . . that is, they first complete a Positive Experience Listing to discover their Greens and Reds. After doing that, they complete the Job Decision Checklist for full-time students, fig. 11-c. This is similar to the Job Decision Checklist for full-time work.

JOB DECISION CHECKLIST
(Full-time student)

Use this Checklist as follow-up to discovering your Greens and Reds. While information about Greens and Reds is foundational, other areas listed below also play an important role in your decision process.

A. List your...

1. INTERESTS AND CONCERNS. Look at your whole life—work, volunteer activities, hobbies, leisure time, etc., not just one area of your life like work or hobbies. What interests you? What needs, problems, issues concern you?

2. DESIRES AND ASPIRATIONS. If you could do what you really wanted, what would you do? Where is your heart? When you are alone—thinking, fantasizing—what do you see yourself doing?

3. KNOWLEDGE STRENGTHS. These are things you know fairly well. Look back over all your experiences—educational, work, volunteer, leisure activities, etc. As you do this, don't compare yourself with other people.

B. MATCH-UP. Match-up is how well each item you listed (A 1, 2, and 3) is compatible with your Greens and what you did in your Positive Experiences. If an item matches up a lot, mark it G (Green); if it matches up some, mark it Y (Yellow); if it matches up very little, mark it R (Red).

If an item seems more personal values/priorities-related, mark it V for values. If an item seems more hobbies-related, mark it A for avocation. Or if an item is Difficult To Classify, mark it DTC.

fig. 11-c

C. JOB OPTION possibilities. In light of the above information, list some specific jobs or potential job opportunities that would best utilize your Greens, and capitalize on your knowledge strengths or other past experiences. Remember your GOAL is to HEAD IN A GREEN DIRECTION; or, said differently, to avoid or minimize using your Reds a lot. You should list at least two job options, or a couple more if you can.

D. SEARCH OUT the field, business or industry that would represent places to look for and/or find a Green-for-you job. Talk to people in that field, business, or industry, asking for their help/advice. Research other resources—books, Internet, etc. Talk to anyone who might know something about the field, business or industry (networking).

E. Decide your MAJOR or field of concentration. What you finally decide should be consistent with your Greens, including some of your Green Interests and Green Job Desires and Aspirations.

During this process, ask God for His Spirit, Wisdom, and Discernment so that you will be most apt to make a God-pleasing decision.

fig. 11-c(2)

Five Case Examples

Case A

Green Focus: Strategy   Major: Physical education

Coach...athletic director

- Playing on championship Little League team
- Making money on, building paper route
- Winning swimming championships
- Coached and played on summer softball programs
- Head counselor at a sports camp
- Soccer, playing halfback...helped the coach
- Getting good grades in 9th grade
- Organized a basketball team; had tryouts;
  almost won the championship; I coached

Case B

Green Focus: Ideas   Major: Biology, Pre-med

- Took walks, looked at ants/bugs through magnifying glass
- Bird watching with my uncle
- Taking care of neighbor's animals
- Being in advanced math classes
- Taking care of puppies when they got sick
- Science and botany classes, always got A's

fig. 11-d

Case C

Green Focus: Ideas   Major: Engineering

- Built a tree fort
- Created and built my own toys
- Designed a special water tank
- Redesigned a mini-bike
- Designed an assembly hookup for a class play
- Helped overhaul a VW engine
- Got interested in solar collectors; designed one
- Getting good grades in math and mechanical drawing

Case D

Green Focus: Relationships   Major: Education

- Directed a play; 'coached' younger kids
- Learned how to make desserts for my family
- Tutored a handicapped neighbor
- Friend and I were social chairpersons of our youth group
- As a senior, helped coach our freshman field hockey team
- Teaching kindergarten class at our church
- Speaking to a Rotary Group

Case E

Green Focus: Tasks   Major: Accounting

- Cleaned our house twice a week; both parents worked full-time
- Organized my desk drawers in my bedroom
- Setting up stereo equipment throughout our house
- I set up and organized a mini-catalog order business
- Stock person at a supermarket; kept shelves neat
- Treasurer for our youth group three years
- I put together a 'family tree' scrapbook in chronological order

fig. 11-d(2)

In fig. 11-d, I have put together, in summary form, the Positive Experiences Listing of five individuals, and potential educational majors based only on their Positive Experiences. These people are in their late teens and early 20s. As we have discussed in previous chapters, an informative resource for narrowing down and deciding future options, in this case an educational major, is someone's Positive Experiences.

Let's assume someone has no idea what he or she wants to do (item A, 2 on the Job Decision Checklist, fig. 11-c), as happens quite often. What I then suggest is to move ahead thoughtfully and carefully, making decisions based on the person's Greens and Reds, plus his or her Interests (item A, 1 on the Job Decision Checklist). Then he or she can make some educational choices that would be most apt to land them in his or her Greens.

Then as he or she goes through his or her educational experience in the days ahead, he or she hopefully will get more direction and sense more what he or she should be doing specifically upon graduation and in that process, gearing his or her courses to a specific field and occupation.

Isn't it interesting? Just a moment ago, I received a call from a first year PhD student . . . looking ahead to three or four more years of education. He said: "I have no idea what I want to do when I get out, or for that matter, what should be my area of concentration."

You already know what I did. I sent him a form to complete his Positive Experiences Listing, and a form to find out items: A-1, Interests, A-2, Desires and Aspirations, and A-3, Knowledge Strengths from the Job Decision Checklist. Sound familiar?

RIGHT MAJOR, BETTER ATTITUDE, BETTER GRADES

Earlier in this chapter we suggested that for many people, the job of student is Yellow or Red, rather than Green. However, when students are majoring in a Green-for-them field (based on what their Positive Experiences are telling them), they should do fairly well, grade-wise. Why? Knowing they are heading in a Green direction, they can better cope with the studying and course preparation, even if it is their Red. They can cope with appropriate discipline and hard work . . . knowing there is light (Green job) at the end of the Red tunnel. And despite the long hours of study, they tend to have a positive attitude.

So a Relationships person may do well grade-wise. If a person's Green skills include helping/encouraging, building relationships, and tutoring, then he or she should do fairly well at college majoring in a field like special needs.

In a nutshell, even though the Student Job Match-up is Red (fig. 11-a), the knowledge that he or she is in the right field should up his or her incentive and motivation to study, even if studying is a Red for him or her. Studying about people with special needs is a world apart from studying computers, accounting, or mathematics.

Whether a person's Green is S, T, I, or R, if he or she majors in the wrong field or area, even if studying is a Green, it will be an uphill battle. Six years after graduating from college, Marge, an education major, completed her Positive Experiences Listing. It pointed out she is an Ideas person, and a Creative/Depictive Artist. Marge is a hands-on artist, not a teacher. Even though she was never that interested in education, with discipline she "stuck it out" and got her degree in education. So even though studying is her Green, she was studying in the wrong field— education. While studying, she had difficulty concentrating, and she would often daydream—using her vivid imagination and creativity to think up arts-related projects that had nothing to do with her major.

GEARING EDUCATION-TRAINING TO GREENS

As we have been seeing, students should be tailoring their education to their Greens and so further develop or improve their Green performance. Of course, occasionally a person takes courses in their Reds, for a variety of reasons. But a person will really learn—change, develop, and improve when what he or she is learning enhances his or her Greens; usually there is limited change-improvement getting training in Reds.

So if someone whose Greens include financial analysis takes courses in cost accounting because he or she is interested in product profitability concepts, then he or she should benefit. That is, use/apply what she learns after the training experience.

But if financial analysis is a person's Reds, he or she may learn well in the classroom, but tend to have little desire or incentive to do it on-goingly in the weeks and months that follow. Learning includes head knowledge, but also it means consistently applying that newfound knowledge and skill down the road.

So a good administrator (his or her Green) taking appropriate administration courses to improve his or her Green skills should expect to perform even better after the training. If instead he or she takes marketing courses, he or she may broaden his or her marketing knowledge, but because his or her heart is in administration, tend not to benefit much in terms of improving his or her marketing (Red) skills.

In a nutshell, people will usually learn best and apply that learning when their education helps them become better in their Greens; learning designed to help them overcome their Reds tends to have less effect on their on-going Red performance.

A CAUTION

People often pursue a major because it is a fast-growing field, or a hot industry. They do this without knowing their Greens and Reds. Please be careful. What is fast-growing now may be slow-growing or dead when someone graduates. What is a down industry now may be an up and coming industry when you graduate. The point is no one really knows.

What we do know is you will be most satisfied and productive in Green work . . . work that capitalizes on your Greens and minimizes using your Reds. Greens and Reds should be foundational information when deciding a major; what is a hot or cold field out there at graduation time or a few years down the road is anyone's guess.

CHAPTER SUMMARY

Our Individual Calling includes using our Greens and some of our Reds. Students (and parents) should form realistic expectations about the role of education in someone's development. Education geared to Greens should benefit students the most; education geared to someone's Red tends to benefit students a lot less.

It all still boils down to: "In your heart of hearts, what is it that you really want to do?" If after completing your Positive Experience Listing, you find out that a job heart aspiration is your Green, then half the battle is over. That is, you have made the crucial decision . . . what you want to do. After that, it is a matter of choosing courses and programs that will build up your knowledge and skills in your chosen field.

While education and training are important, they are not a god. School grades are not a god. Degrees and certificates are not god. Our most important knowledge is knowing the one and only true God and that He values/cherishes our love for Him. "Knowledge puffs up, but love builds up. The man who thinks he knows something does not yet know as he ought to know. But the man who loves God is known by God" (1 Corinthians 8:1b-3).

BOOK SUMMARY

REVIEW

As I have been writing this book, I have tried to keep several themes in mind. They include:

- That we should view *success* as God views success, not as man views success.
- We are here on earth to *please* and *glorify* God in everything we do and say.
- That we need to make *decisions* with God in mind, and our *thoughts* imbued with Scripture's instructions for us to obey.
- That God desires we *walk closely* with Him; and when a person is in a job that gives a sense of accomplishment and satisfaction, then there is the potential for a close, intimate walk with God.
- That knowledge of a person's *Greens* and *Reds* contributes to a person finding what would be a Green or Red job for him . . . Green being a major source for a satisfying and meaningful-to-him-or-her job.
- That an *organized* approach to decision making includes at least three things: knowledge of a person's Greens and Reds, his or her Values-Priorities, and his or her Life Purpose and Goals.

HOW GOD VIEWS SELF-CONFIDENCE

We have dealt generally with our Universal Calling, and more specifically with our Individual Calling. Right now, you may be in Group A or Group B. Group A is very confident. People among them know their Greens and Reds, and their Values-Priorities are pinpointed specifically, and their Life Purpose is clearly defined. And they know with certainty the two or three job or career options potentially right for them. In a word, everything is crystal clear. In fact, presently they have no desire to do anything other than what they are doing now.

Group B is less confident. Although still unsure, they have some handle on their Greens and Reds, are still foggy about their Values-Priorities, and their Life Purpose is still in the thinking stage. It has been like "pulling teeth" trying to come up with even one, let alone two job or career options that may be possibilities for them. What they do now is at best a Yellow job, most likely a Red job. Right now, despite their best efforts at "clearing the fog," things are still unclear.

Now which Group do you think is most apt to be dependent on God right now, A or B?

Yes, we know what the answer should be—both A & B. But the right answer is usually Group B. Their lack of confidence and decision uncertainty sees them looking to God and being deadly serious about needing and wanting God's help. Do you think God is pleased by their attitude and actions? You bet He is.

Let's look at Group A. Over the years, people have confided in me that when things are going well in their lives, they tend to ignore God . . . not outwardly, but inwardly. Outwardly, everything looks OK, giving the appearance that they are doing well on the job, busy in their church and communities, giving the appearance of success, etc.

But inwardly, it's a different story . . . they feel distant from God. They know this because during moments of reflection, the Holy Spirit convicts them for not stopping long enough to pray or study Scripture, and forgetting to seek God during the course of the day: "Seek first his kingdom and his righteousness . . ." (Matthew 6:33).

There is confidence and then there is confidence—a right kind of confidence and a wrong kind of confidence. People 100% sure or confident of their decision-making ability, their decisions, their life direction, the choices they have made, etc. turn me off. In my view, this is the wrong kind of confidence. They talk and act as though they have an answer to every issue or problem on this earth. I tend not to be drawn to such people. In fact, I have to work hard at liking them.

People less confident, say but 80% sure or confident of their decision-making ability, life direction, etc. turn me on; I am drawn to them. They are not sure; they are uncertain. In my view, this is a right kind of confidence.

I believe God is pleased when we have the right kind of confidence; we are confident to a point, but "humbly" confident. We are sure, yet not totally sure. I call this *decision uncertainty*. I believe decision uncertainty pleases God because it is then we "prone-to-ignore-God people" are more apt to depend on God. "But this happened that we might not rely on ourselves but God . . ." (2 Corinthians 1:9).

All said differently, our total, 100% confidence is in God Himself; we believe in Him unswervingly; we trust to the end that His Holy Spirit will influence what we do. On the other hand, we are less confident of our own decision making, so uncertainty characterizes decision making.

And I believe this is the way it should be because it causes us to be in a "dependent-on-Him" mode all the time. Otherwise, if we were in a "decision certain" mode, we would depend on fancy decision making models, or "techniques" for Finding Our Calling . . . rather than depend on God Himself.

People with a degree of uncertainty in themselves and their decisions usually are quietly confident, quietly active in service to Him. "Make it your ambition to lead a quiet life . . . so that your daily life may win the respect of outsider . . ." (1 Thessalonians 4:11-12).

Quiet. Sh-h-h-h-h. Turn it off. Listen. There are still sounds, but try concentrating on God—who He is, His goodness, His love, all His provisions for you, etc. Then out of nowhere comes an idea; your heart warms to it. It keeps "bubbling up." "Is that what I should do?" you ask.

You check out your idea with your Positive Experiences Listing; it is a Green possibility. Then over the next few days, your Life Purpose begins to clarify. You use the Job Decision Checklist to guide your next decisions and actions. You ask: "Could the 'Sprinkle Down Concept' be in operation?" With a deep sense of gratitude and humility, you think, "Yes, I am quite certain God, via His Holy Spirit, planted (sprinkled down) that seed thought. Thank you, Lord."

"In quietness and trust is your strength." Isaiah 30:15
"May the God of peace . . . equip you with everything good for doing his will, and may He work in us what is pleasing to him . . . ."
Hebrews 13:20-21

"May God himself, the God of peace, sanctify you through and through. May your whole spirit, soul and body be kept blameless at the coming of our Lord Jesus Christ. The one who calls you is faithful, and he will do it."
1 Thessalonians 5:23-24

He calls us . . . He is faithful . . . He will do it. God equips, He is at work in us; God Himself will keep us "blameless at the coming of our Lord Jesus Christ." What is Green with God? Being a "walking-close-to-Him" believer. What's Red with God? Being a "walking-far-from-Him" believer. God's call is to the former, not latter. That is success, in God's eyes.

OPTIONAL READING

One of my favorite Scriptures is John 15, the Vine/branch allegory. I have written the following about it . . . to either help you gain perspective and/or encourage you. Here goes.

Fruit grows quietly in orchards. If you stood silently in an orchard, you would not hear fruit growing on branches. The branch does its work quietly and effectively. The branch depends on the main stem for life-giving energy and support. The resulting fruit is not consumed by either the branch or main stem but by external entities. In fact, the branch really does not know who benefits the most from its harvested crops. The branch is really a go-between instrument between its Energy Source and pickers/users.

This book has been for people who want to work quietly and effectively in the "vineyards and trenches" of life. They are what I call "behind-the-scenes" leaders who neither need nor want lots of public acclaim. An occa-, sional, well-meant "thank you" is their biggest reward.

226

Their results are barely visible or measurable. You would have to sit a long time in their "orchards" of life before noticing fruit ripening from their labors. Besides, it is seasonal "picking" . . . lot of blood, sweat, and tears preceded their "little contribution" to the Owner's final crop.

Funny thing about the main stem. He is really a Teacher, and He teaches in bits and pieces. He never gives the overview or the final end goal. So branches have to come to Him often, consistently, hourly, and moment by moment. His teachings are so radically different it takes a lifetime to just begin to grasp their meaning and significance. And this Teacher has experienced what He is teaching. He even weeps when branches turn rebellious. He concentrates on one or a few branches at a time, rather than scattering His efforts.

This book has been for people serious about Christianity, who revere their Teacher and His Teachings. Their relationship to Him is personal and special. While they don't always feel like His student/disciple, or even always feel His presence, they persevere. They have confidence in their Teacher. On the other hand, they are uncertain of what He may teach them next or what their next "assignment" might be.

One more "funny thing." The Owner and "Main Stem" are like one entity. They also admit the existence of a Third Person who comes and goes like the orchard's wind. He too forms part of that One Entity. All Three are heard to talk a lot about the branch's heart—pure or deceitful, clean or impure, compassionate or merciless, caring or insensitive. They also say they can evaluate the heart's motives.

I hope this book has heightened your view of God, and deepened your walk with Him. Our Calling is to God. May through His eyes, and the enabling of His Holy Spirit, your future will be known enough for you to be heading in a Green direction, and leading you to be successful in His eyes.

QUESTIONS FOR DISCUSSION

Look at these questions when you finish reading a chapter. They are designed to (1) be thought provoking and (2) encourage application of ideas in real-life situations. These questions are helpful answered either individually or in discussion groups—where the discussion leader uses the questions as discussion starters. In either case, an individual, discussion leader, or discussion group may decide to concentrate on a few selected questions instead of answering all of them. Do what meets needs best.

CHAPTER 1

1. The ultimate aim of every believer should be to please God at all times.
    a. What does it mean to please God?
    b. What does pleasing God include? See Hebrews 11:5-6, Galatians 1:10.

2. What attitudes please God? Displease God? See Philippians 2:5-8, 21 as well as other Scripture that comes to mind.

3. In your opinion, what are the two things a believer should do each day to live a God-pleasing life?
    a. What are the main obstacles facing a person striving to do these two things each day?

4. Universal Calling includes what should be a believer's priority relationship (to walk closely with God), priority commitment (to love God and neighbor), and primary motive (to glorify God). How should believers go about:
    a. Making their walk-with-God their priority relationship?
    b. Keeping to-love-God-and-neighbor their primary commitment?
    c. Maintaining to-glorify-God their primary motive?

CHAPTER 2

1. God instructs a person to "find satisfaction in his toilsome labor" (Ecclesiastes 5:18-20).
    a. According to Ecclesiastes 3:24-26, in addition to the gift of job satisfaction (v. 24), what else can someone who is trying to please God expect from Him (v. 26)?
    b. Why are these promises (v. 26) important to someone striving to please God?

2. The 6th principle behind the Green Light Concept is "Decision Latitude"—that God gives a person both the freedom and responsibility to figure out his or her future and that God's Plan is to help that person make a best decision.
    a. Do you believe God gives a person 'Decision Latitude' when making job choices? Give reasons for your conclusion.

3. Below are three benefits to a person for knowing their Greens, Yellows, and Reds. Describe how each one may contribute to their ability to make God-pleasing decisions.
    a. Form realistic (and accurate) expectations.
    b. Erase false guilt.
    c. Understand the impact (of Greens and Reds) on relationships.

CHAPTER 3

1. Figures 3-c to 3-f point out significant differences in people's Greens—focus, skills, satisfaction, and characteristics. How might this information help people . . .
    a. Relate to each other better?
    b. Work as a team?
    c. When making job assignments to people?

2. Do you believe that God is the only One who completely understands a person? If yes, why? If no, why?
    a. What are the ramifications of your views/conclusions in your understanding of yourself? Other people?

3. Why should a person rely on his or her Positive Experiences Listing when discovering his or her Greens? Why is this often difficult to do?

4. All people should value people and view them as God's creation and gifts to them. Why do some people, regardless of their Strategy, Tasks, Ideas, or Relationships tendencies, seem to do a better job at this than others?
    a. How can someone consistently hold to a "value people" mentality during life's ups and downs?

5. What is the major point of the "washing dishes" scenario?
    a. Do you believe a person should temper his or her (Green) tendencies in light of his or her circumstances and situational realities? If yes, why? How? If no, why?

CHAPTER 4

1. What does the principle "Delight yourself in the Lord" (Ps. 37:4) mean to you? Why is this principle foundational to one's Calling?

2. List several potential "Spiritual heart desires" (Ps. 37:4) possibilities for you or anyone else to consider. How should a person go about deciding which ones to embrace and live by?

3. Why should a person's Job heart desires be developed only after deciding his or her Spiritual heart desires? What are the benefits?

4. In your own words, describe the Bubble Up Concept and Sprinkle Down Concept.
   a. Why should these Concepts be affirming and encouraging to someone?

5. In your opinion, how should a believer deal with his or her heart condition in light of Jeremiah 17:9: "The heart is deceitful above all things."

CHAPTER 5

1. Why consider three areas—Job, Values/Priorities, and Life Purpose and Goals, rather than just one area—Job in the Finding Your Calling process?

2. Reread Ecclesiastes 7:14; 9:1; 11:5. Why is a deep faith and unwavering trust in God so essential while (1) planning for the future and (2) dealing with life's realities, including ups and downs?

3. What is meant by Job Match-up? What is its goal?
   a. Does the concept of "fitting the job to the person" make sense to you? Why or why not?

4. Why should a person clarify his or her Values/Priorities (Spiritual and Other Life Values)? What is gained by doing this? Lost by not doing it?

False Self		
<u>Will</u> Control	Anger	Lust Sloth Anger
<u>Memory</u> Image	Shame	Pride Deceit Envy
<u>Intellect</u> Security	Fear	Avarice Gluttony Fear

True Self		
<u>Love</u>	Trust	Compassion Gentleness Love
<u>Hope</u>	Honesty	Humility Truthfulness Goodness
<u>Faith</u>	Courage	Self Control Joy Faithfulness

5. In your opinion, what is success in (1) God's eyes and (2) the world's eyes? How should a person go about formulating what success is for him or her?

6. A person's Life Purpose includes helping people. How can the concept of helping people directly or indirectly benefit someone when developing a Life Purpose?

CHAPTER 6

1. In your opinion, how should a person go about dealing with the stumbling blocks that affect him or her directly? What is the one thing he or she must do? Must not do?

2. Stumbling block 3. I-want-to-help-people mentality . . . may be easy to agree with intellectually, but difficult to put into practice. Why do you think that is so?

3. A person is using his or her God-given Greens in his or her full-time job . . . and while doing so, works mainly by himself or herself. He or she feels they are "Living Out Their Calling" except in one area, helping people. If they asked you for your advice, what would you say to them?

4. Reread Philippians 4:13. What is your interpretation of this verse? Regardless of a person's particular interpretation, what is the key promise of this verse? How can a person consistently implement this promise?

5. Why may responsible believers succumb to large or increasingly large monthly financial obligations that often dictate their decisions and lifestyle?
   a. Can this be avoided? If yes, why? How? If no, why?

CHAPTER 7

1. Why do most people procrastinate when faced with a Red-for-them task?
   a. What are other reasons a person may procrastinate?
   b. In your opinion, what is the solution to the procrastination issue?

2. Give reasons people should not avoid responsibilities requiring them to do Red work, along with doing Green work?

3. In your own words, describe the Spill Over Concept. How does it help people do Red-for-them tasks?

4. In your opinion, why does God give people Reds?

5. How should a person go about doing a Red-for-him-or-her task well (B+ or A level work) in light of situational pressures and deadlines?
   a. How can he or she maintain a God-pleasing attitude while doing it?

6. What is the main thing you learned in this chapter? How can you apply it?

CHAPTER 8

1. In your opinion, why would someone stay in a Red job, knowing full well the negative consequences of Red work (See again fig. 2-b, By-Products), including on his or her walk with God? Do you think God would be pleased with his or her decision? If yes, why? If no, why not?

2. Do you feel there are valid, God-pleasing reasons for someone to remain in a Red-for- him-or-her job longer than 18 months, even indefinitely? Give reasons for your conclusions.

3. Do you believe job contentment is God-pleasing (Recall the example, "In your heart of hearts, what is it that you want to do?" Answer: "All I want is to do my best where I am now. I am so fortunate.")? If yes, why? If no, why?

4. Suppose a person decides to remain in a low-paying field and Green job, rather than go into a higher-paying field and Red job. What Values/Priorities may help him or her during the inevitable financially rough days ahead?

5. List what you feel are the three most important reasons for a person to be in a Green job rather than Red job.

CHAPTER 9

1. Describe the Carry-Over principle.
   a. Generally speaking, how are Attitudes, Relationships, and Action influenced by:
      (1). A Green job?
      (2). A Red job?

2. Do you believe home is often a testing ground for living/behaving Christianly? If yes, why? If no, why?

3. In your opinion, why is it often difficult to have a "serving others" attitude at home? Is that the way it should be? Why?
   a. How should someone go about trying to maintain a "serving others" attitude at home?

4. React to the statement: "It is virtually impossible for someone in Red work to have a servant's heart reasonably consistently." Give reasons for your conclusions.

5. In your view, what are God-pleasing attitude and character qualities that contribute to positive relationships and a warm/caring environment in a home?
   a. In your view, what attitudes most often contribute to relationship breakdowns? How can such attitudes be overcome?

6. What is the major theme(s) running through this chapter? How can a person apply it (them) day-in, day-out?

CHAPTER 10

1. In your opinion, is doing volunteer work a privilege? If yes, why? If no, why?
   a. What situational factors (job life, home life, church life, relationships) may influence your opinion?
   b. What are good reasons for volunteering? Poor reasons?

2. What are the essential attitude requirements of a volunteer? How can volunteers encourage one another?

3. How does a Green job or Red job at work affect people's willingness to do volunteer work? Why is this so?

4. In your view, what are spiritual gifts? What is their purpose? Do you feel they are identifiable? If yes, why? If no, why?
   a. What role, if any, do you feel spiritual gifts play as people function as volunteers in their churches?

5. How should a person go about deciding what to do as a volunteer in his or her church? How should he or she put his or her decision into action?

CHAPTER 11

1. Do you think it is realistic and practical to view what full-time students do as their Student Job? Give reasons for your conclusion.
   a. How might such a view help a student? Be a hindrance to a student?

2. What student attitudes contribute to good grades? Poor grades?

3. In all probability, all students have to take courses that are both Red-for-them and in which they have little or no interest. What principles should they keep in mind during such times in order to be God-honoring, God-glorifying students?

4. Why should a person aim to gear his or her education-training to his or her Greens?
   a. What are the advantages and benefits?
   b. Why are people most apt to use/implement such education-training?

BOOK SUMMARY

1. Describe what "decision uncertainty" means. Do you feel such a concept contributes to a person relying more often and consistently on God? If yes, why? If no, why?

2. Isaiah 56:8 says: "'For my thoughts are not your thoughts, neither are your ways my ways,' declares the Lord." How can this verse apply . . .
   a. During the Finding your Calling process?
   b. While Living Out your Calling?

3. John 15:5 says: "If a man remains [abides] in me and I in him, he will bear much fruit; apart from me [Jesus] you can do nothing."
   a. According to this verse, why "remain close" to Jesus (Universal Calling—close, personal relationship with Jesus)?

4. What do you think is the major theme/message of this book? Give reasons for your conclusions.
   a. How can it (theme/message) be applied consistently in a person's life for them to live God-pleasing lives?

APPENDIX B

SATISFACTION

Here are some examples of what people say about a Positive Experience when asked: "What was satisfying (or fulfilling) to you about that Positive Experience"?

S STRATEGY	T TASKS
Satisfying: *"Overcoming the obstacles, the competing, winning, pushing myself to the limit."* This means a person needs to WIN or surmount SEVERE DIFFICULTIES to feel satisfied.	Satisfying: *"Becoming proficient at it, doing it properly...solving problems and making it right...improving it."* This means a person needs to make it BETTER or do it better/faster to feel satisfied.
Satisfying: *"Being in front of large audiences...being in charge, being totally responsible for whatever happened."* This means a person needs to be IN CHARGE or IN FRONT of audiences to feel satisfied.	Satisfying: *"Getting it right, making it orderly...it came out looking right—neat, polished, perfect."* This means a person needs to shape up or CLEAN UP an area, or CORRECT flaws to feel satisfied.
Satisfying: *"Noticing progress right away, seeing measurable results...numbers tell a story, it's in black and white."* This means a person needs to see IMMEDIATE progress and results quickly to feel satisfied.	Satisfying: *"Making own decisions, being independent, no one interfered, so the job was done right."* This means a person needs to make decisions WITHOUT RELYING a lot on others and do something RIGHT to feel satisfied.

I IDEAS	R RELATIONSHIPS
Satisfying: *"Feeling like I was on a treasure hunt and discovering new truths, facts...the learning and understanding it...becoming engrossed in the process."* This means a person needs to acquire knowledge, expertise, COMPREHENSION to feel satisfied. Satisfying: *"The creative process, seeing it go from nothing to something...expressing myself...making, producing beauty and orderliness."* This means a person needs to MAKE or FORM a visible or audible end-product/end-expression to feel satisfied.	Satisfying: *"Their approval and compliments...their immediate acceptance...noticing their change, frowns changing to smiles."* This means a person needs to be appreciated, AFFIRMED to feel satisfied. Satisfying: *"Doing it together, the camaraderie...developing relationships, simply helping people...that everyone pitched in...being part of a cooperative effort."* This means a person needs to do things WITH OTHERS, HELPING OUT to feel satisfied. Satisfying: *"It was unique, one of a kind...doing something others normally do not do...it was new and different...being their special helper and confidant(e)."* This means a person needs to be SPECIAL to someone and/or do something different, DISTINCTIVE to feel satisfied.